Sales Strategy
Complete Self-Assessment Guide

The guidance in this Self-Assessment is based on Sales Strategy, ... practices and standards in business process architecture, design and quality management. The guidance is also based on the professional judgment of the individual collaborators listed in the Acknowledgments.

Notice of rights

Trademarks

Table of Contents

About The Art of Service

The Art of Service, Business Process Architects since 2000, is dedicated to helping stakeholders achieve excellence.

Defining, designing, creating, and implementing a process to solve a stakeholders challenge or meet an objective is the most valuable role... In EVERY group, company, organization and department.

Unless you're talking a one-time, single-use project, there should be a process. Whether that process is managed and implemented by humans, AI, or a combination of the two, it needs to be designed by someone with a complex enough perspective to ask the right questions.

Someone capable of asking the right questions and step back and say, 'What are we really trying to accomplish here? And is there a different way to look at it?'

With The Art of Service's Standard Requirements Self-Assessments, we empower people who can do just that — whether their title is marketer, entrepreneur, manager, salesperson, consultant, Business Process Manager, executive assistant, IT Manager, CIO etc... —they are the people who rule the future. They are people who watch the process as it happens, and ask the right questions to make the process work better.

Contact us when you need any support with this Self-Assessment and any help with templates, blue-prints and examples of standard documents you might need:

http://theartofservice.com
service@theartofservice.com

Included Resources - how to access

Included with your purchase of the book is the Sales Strategy

Self-Assessment Spreadsheet Dashboard which contains all questions and Self-Assessment areas and auto-generates insights, graphs, and project RACI planning - all with examples to get you started right away.

How? Simply send an email to
access@theartofservice.com
with this books' title in the subject to get the Sales Strategy Self Assessment Tool right away.

You will receive the following contents with New and Updated specific criteria:

- The latest quick edition of the book in PDF

- The latest complete edition of the book in PDF, which criteria correspond to the criteria in...

- The Self-Assessment Excel Dashboard, and...

- Example pre-filled Self-Assessment Excel Dashboard to get familiar with results generation

- In-depth specific Checklists covering the topic

- Project management checklists and templates to assist with implementation

INCLUDES LIFETIME SELF ASSESSMENT UPDATES

Every self assessment comes with Lifetime Updates and Lifetime Free Updated Books. Lifetime Updates is an industry-first feature which allows you to receive verified self assessment updates, ensuring you always have the most accurate information at your fingertips.

Get it now- you will be glad you did - do it now, before you forget.

Send an email to **access@theartofservice.com** with this books' title in the subject to get the Sales Strategy Self Assessment Tool right away.

Purpose of this Self-Assessment

This Self-Assessment has been developed to improve understanding of the requirements and elements of Sales Strategy, based on best practices and standards in business process architecture, design and quality management.

It is designed to allow for a rapid Self-Assessment to determine how closely existing management practices and procedures correspond to the elements of the Self-Assessment.

The criteria of requirements and elements of Sales Strategy have been rephrased in the format of a Self-Assessment questionnaire, with a seven-criterion scoring system, as explained in this document.

In this format, even with limited background knowledge of Sales Strategy, a manager can quickly review existing operations to determine how they measure up to the standards. This in turn can serve as the starting point of a 'gap analysis' to identify management tools or system elements that might usefully be implemented in the organization to help improve overall performance.

How to use the Self-Assessment

On the following pages are a series of questions to identify to what extent your Sales Strategy initiative is complete in comparison to the requirements set in standards.

To facilitate answering the questions, there is a space in front of each question to enter a score on a scale of '1' to '5'.

1 Strongly Disagree

2 Disagree

3 Neutral

4 Agree

5 Strongly Agree

Read the question and rate it with the following in front of mind:

'In my belief,
the answer to this question is clearly defined'.

There are two ways in which you can choose to interpret this statement;
1. how aware are you that the answer to the question is clearly defined
2. for more in-depth analysis you can choose to gather evidence and confirm the answer to the question. This obviously will take more time, most Self-Assessment users opt for the first way to interpret the question and dig deeper later on based on the outcome of the overall Self-Assessment.

A score of '1' would mean that the answer is not clear at all, where a '5' would mean the answer is crystal clear and defined. Leave emtpy when the question is not applicable or you don't want to answer it, you can skip it without affecting your score. Write your score in the space provided.

After you have responded to all the appropriate statements in each section, compute your average score for that section, using the formula provided, and round to the nearest tenth. Then transfer to the corresponding spoke in the Sales Strategy Scorecard on the second next page of the Self-Assessment.

Your completed Sales Strategy Scorecard will give you a clear presentation of which Sales Strategy areas need attention.

Sales Strategy
Scorecard Example

Example of how the finalized Scorecard can look like:

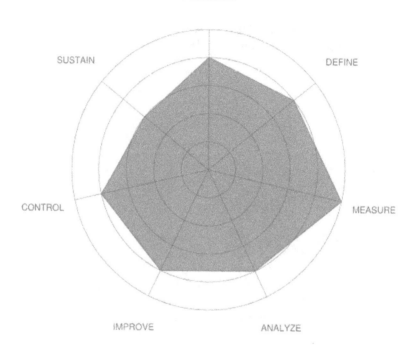

Sales Strategy Scorecard

Your Scores:

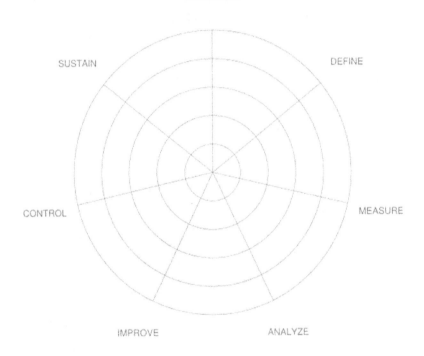

BEGINNING OF THE SELF-ASSESSMENT:

CRITERION #1: RECOGNIZE

INTENT: Be aware of the need for change. Recognize that there is an unfavorable variation, problem or symptom.

In my belief, the answer to this question is clearly defined:

5 Strongly Agree

4 Agree

3 Neutral

2 Disagree

1 Strongly Disagree

1. Who else hopes to benefit from it?
<--- Score

2. Are losses recognized in a timely manner?
<--- Score

3. Which needs are not included or involved?
<--- Score

4. Will sales strategy deliverables need to be tested and, if so, by whom?
<--- Score

5. How many trainings, in total, are needed?
<--- Score

6. How are you going to measure success?
<--- Score

7. Are you dealing with any of the same issues today as yesterday? What can you do about this?
<--- Score

8. Are controls defined to recognize and contain problems?
<--- Score

9. What problems are you facing and how do you consider sales strategy will circumvent those obstacles?
<--- Score

10. Do you have/need 24-hour access to key personnel?
<--- Score

11. What does sales strategy success mean to the stakeholders?
<--- Score

12. How much are sponsors, customers, partners, stakeholders involved in sales strategy? In other words, what are the risks, if sales strategy does not deliver successfully?
<--- Score

13. How do you assess your sales strategy workforce capability and capacity needs, including skills, competencies, and staffing levels?
<--- Score

14. What do employees need in the short term?
<--- Score

15. How are training requirements identified?
<--- Score

16. Does sales strategy create potential expectations in other areas that need to be recognized and considered?
<--- Score

17. What tools and technologies are needed for a custom sales strategy project?
<--- Score

18. How do you take a forward-looking perspective in identifying sales strategy research related to market response and models?
<--- Score

19. Is the quality assurance team identified?
<--- Score

20. What extra resources will you need?
<--- Score

21. What is the problem and/or vulnerability?
<--- Score

22. Who needs to know?

<--- Score

23. What should be considered when identifying available resources, constraints, and deadlines?
<--- Score

24. How do you recognize an objection?
<--- Score

25. Think about the people you identified for your sales strategy project and the project responsibilities you would assign to them, what kind of training do you think they would need to perform these responsibilities effectively?
<--- Score

26. Whom do you really need or want to serve?
<--- Score

27. To what extent does each concerned units management team recognize sales strategy as an effective investment?
<--- Score

28. What sales strategy events should you attend?
<--- Score

29. What training and capacity building actions are needed to implement proposed reforms?
<--- Score

30. Do you recognize sales strategy achievements?
<--- Score

31. Who needs what information?
<--- Score

32. Do you know what you need to know about sales strategy?
<--- Score

33. How do you recognize an sales strategy objection?
<--- Score

34. Are problem definition and motivation clearly presented?
<--- Score

35. How does it fit into your organizational needs and tasks?
<--- Score

36. What are the stakeholder objectives to be achieved with sales strategy?
<--- Score

37. Are there recognized sales strategy problems?
<--- Score

38. Which issues are too important to ignore?
<--- Score

39. Are there any revenue recognition issues?
<--- Score

40. For your sales strategy project, identify and describe the business environment, is there more than one layer to the business environment?
<--- Score

41. As a sponsor, customer or management, how important is it to meet goals, objectives?

<--- Score

42. What creative shifts do you need to take?
<--- Score

43. What resources or support might you need?
<--- Score

44. What sales strategy problem should be solved?
<--- Score

45. What are your needs in relation to sales strategy skills, labor, equipment, and markets?
<--- Score

46. What needs to be done?
<--- Score

47. Is it clear when you think of the day ahead of you what activities and tasks you need to complete?
<--- Score

48. Why the need?
<--- Score

49. Would you recognize a threat from the inside?
<--- Score

50. What are the clients issues and concerns?
<--- Score

51. Did you miss any major sales strategy issues?
<--- Score

52. What are the expected benefits of sales strategy to the stakeholder?

<--- Score

53. What are the minority interests and what amount of minority interests can be recognized?
<--- Score

54. Are there sales strategy problems defined?
<--- Score

55. What prevents you from making the changes you know will make you a more effective sales strategy leader?
<--- Score

56. What else needs to be measured?
<--- Score

57. Will it solve real problems?
<--- Score

58. What situation(s) led to this sales strategy Self Assessment?
<--- Score

59. Are your goals realistic? Do you need to redefine your problem? Perhaps the problem has changed or maybe you have reached your goal and need to set a new one?
<--- Score

60. How do you identify subcontractor relationships?
<--- Score

61. What do you need to start doing?
<--- Score

62. Will new equipment/products be required to facilitate sales strategy delivery, for example is new software needed?
<--- Score

63. What is the recognized need?
<--- Score

64. What sales strategy capabilities do you need?
<--- Score

65. Who should resolve the sales strategy issues?
<--- Score

66. Are there any specific expectations or concerns about the sales strategy team, sales strategy itself?
<--- Score

67. Who defines the rules in relation to any given issue?
<--- Score

68. What is the extent or complexity of the sales strategy problem?
<--- Score

69. Where do you need to exercise leadership?
<--- Score

70. What activities does the governance board need to consider?
<--- Score

71. Who are your key stakeholders who need to sign off?
<--- Score

72. How can auditing be a preventative security measure?
<--- Score

73. Are employees recognized or rewarded for performance that demonstrates the highest levels of integrity?
<--- Score

74. To what extent would your organization benefit from being recognized as a award recipient?
<--- Score

75. What is the smallest subset of the problem you can usefully solve?
<--- Score

76. Can management personnel recognize the monetary benefit of sales strategy?
<--- Score

77. What needs to stay?
<--- Score

78. Do you need to avoid or amend any sales strategy activities?
<--- Score

79. Is the need for organizational change recognized?
<--- Score

80. Where is training needed?
<--- Score

81. Does the problem have ethical dimensions?

<--- Score

82. What vendors make products that address the sales strategy needs?
<--- Score

83. What sales strategy coordination do you need?
<--- Score

84. Looking at each person individually – does every one have the qualities which are needed to work in this group?
<--- Score

85. What are the sales strategy resources needed?
<--- Score

86. Does your organization need more sales strategy education?
<--- Score

87. Who needs to know about sales strategy?
<--- Score

88. Have you identified your sales strategy key performance indicators?
<--- Score

89. What are the timeframes required to resolve each of the issues/problems?
<--- Score

90. What would happen if sales strategy weren't done?
<--- Score

91. How do you identify the kinds of information that you will need?
<--- Score

92. How are the sales strategy's objectives aligned to the group's overall stakeholder strategy?
<--- Score

93. What information do users need?
<--- Score

94. Are employees recognized for desired behaviors?
<--- Score

95. Will a response program recognize when a crisis occurs and provide some level of response?
<--- Score

96. When a sales strategy manager recognizes a problem, what options are available?
<--- Score

Add up total points for this section:
_____ = Total points for this section

Divided by: _____ (number of statements answered) = _____ Average score for this section

Transfer your score to the sales strategy Index at the beginning of the Self-Assessment.

CRITERION #2: DEFINE:

INTENT: Formulate the stakeholder problem. Define the problem, needs and objectives.

In my belief, the answer to this question is clearly defined:

5 Strongly Agree

4 Agree

3 Neutral

2 Disagree

1 Strongly Disagree

1. Does the team have regular meetings?
<--- Score

2. Are team charters developed?
<--- Score

3. How do you gather requirements?
<--- Score

4. Are the sales strategy requirements testable?
<--- Score

5. What is out-of-scope initially?
<--- Score

6. What are the Roles and Responsibilities for each team member and its leadership? Where is this documented?
<--- Score

7. Are stakeholder processes mapped?
<--- Score

8. What are the tasks and definitions?
<--- Score

9. What is a worst-case scenario for losses?
<--- Score

10. Are roles and responsibilities formally defined?
<--- Score

11. What scope to assess?
<--- Score

12. Is there regularly 100% attendance at the team meetings? If not, have appointed substitutes attended to preserve cross-functionality and full representation?
<--- Score

13. What is the scope of the sales strategy effort?
<--- Score

14. Will a sales strategy production readiness review

be required?
<--- Score

15. What baselines are required to be defined and managed?
<--- Score

16. Has a high-level 'as is' process map been completed, verified and validated?
<--- Score

17. What is the context?
<--- Score

18. Has the improvement team collected the 'voice of the customer' (obtained feedback – qualitative and quantitative)?
<--- Score

19. Has everyone on the team, including the team leaders, been properly trained?
<--- Score

20. Is data collected and displayed to better understand customer(s) critical needs and requirements.
<--- Score

21. Are resources adequate for the scope?
<--- Score

22. How does the sales strategy manager ensure against scope creep?
<--- Score

23. Have specific policy objectives been defined?

<--- Score

24. Are accountability and ownership for sales strategy clearly defined?
<--- Score

25. What scope do you want your strategy to cover?
<--- Score

26. Is the current 'as is' process being followed? If not, what are the discrepancies?
<--- Score

27. What is the scope of the sales strategy work?
<--- Score

28. What are the core elements of the sales strategy business case?
<--- Score

29. What are the requirements for audit information?
<--- Score

30. When is the estimated completion date?
<--- Score

31. What are the dynamics of the communication plan?
<--- Score

32. What are the boundaries of the scope? What is in bounds and what is not? What is the start point? What is the stop point?
<--- Score

33. Are there any constraints known that bear on the

ability to perform sales strategy work? How is the team addressing them?

<--- Score

34. What defines best in class?

<--- Score

35. Has the sales strategy work been fairly and/ or equitably divided and delegated among team members who are qualified and capable to perform the work? Has everyone contributed?

<--- Score

36. What information do you gather?

<--- Score

37. When is/was the sales strategy start date?

<--- Score

38. How do you manage scope?

<--- Score

39. How are consistent sales strategy definitions important?

<--- Score

40. Have the customer needs been translated into specific, measurable requirements? How?

<--- Score

41. Is there any additional sales strategy definition of success?

<--- Score

42. How is the team tracking and documenting its work?

<--- Score

43. Is there a critical path to deliver sales strategy results?
<--- Score

44. Will team members perform sales strategy work when assigned and in a timely fashion?
<--- Score

45. Who are the sales strategy improvement team members, including Management Leads and Coaches?
<--- Score

46. How would you define the culture at your organization, how susceptible is it to sales strategy changes?
<--- Score

47. How often are the team meetings?
<--- Score

48. Is sales strategy currently on schedule according to the plan?
<--- Score

49. If substitutes have been appointed, have they been briefed on the sales strategy goals and received regular communications as to the progress to date?
<--- Score

50. How and when will the baselines be defined?
<--- Score

51. Is there a completed SIPOC representation,

describing the Suppliers, Inputs, Process, Outputs, and Customers?
<--- Score

52. How do you catch sales strategy definition inconsistencies?
<--- Score

53. Is the team equipped with available and reliable resources?
<--- Score

54. Are audit criteria, scope, frequency and methods defined?
<--- Score

55. What is the scope?
<--- Score

56. What knowledge or experience is required?
<--- Score

57. What sort of initial information to gather?
<--- Score

58. Do the problem and goal statements meet the SMART criteria (specific, measurable, attainable, relevant, and time-bound)?
<--- Score

59. Do you have a sales strategy success story or case study ready to tell and share?
<--- Score

60. Is the team adequately staffed with the desired cross-functionality? If not, what additional resources

are available to the team?
<--- Score

61. What sales strategy services do you require?
<--- Score

62. Is there a clear sales strategy case definition?
<--- Score

63. What critical content must be communicated –
who, what, when, where, and how?
<--- Score

64. What is the definition of sales strategy excellence?
<--- Score

65. What gets examined?
<--- Score

66. Is sales strategy linked to key stakeholder goals
and objectives?
<--- Score

67. What key stakeholder process output measure(s)
does sales strategy leverage and how?
<--- Score

68. Who is gathering sales strategy information?
<--- Score

69. How do you think the partners involved in sales
strategy would have defined success?
<--- Score

70. Who defines (or who defined) the rules and roles?
<--- Score

71. What are the compelling stakeholder reasons for embarking on sales strategy?
<--- Score

72. Who approved the sales strategy scope?
<--- Score

73. How do you manage unclear sales strategy requirements?
<--- Score

74. How do you gather the stories?
<--- Score

75. When are meeting minutes sent out? Who is on the distribution list?
<--- Score

76. What specifically is the problem? Where does it occur? When does it occur? What is its extent?
<--- Score

77. What is the worst case scenario?
<--- Score

78. Are improvement team members fully trained on sales strategy?
<--- Score

79. What is the definition of success?
<--- Score

80. Has a sales strategy requirement not been met?
<--- Score

81. Is the team sponsored by a champion or stakeholder leader?
<--- Score

82. How do you manage changes in sales strategy requirements?
<--- Score

83. How will the sales strategy team and the group measure complete success of sales strategy?
<--- Score

84. What are the record-keeping requirements of sales strategy activities?
<--- Score

85. What customer feedback methods were used to solicit their input?
<--- Score

86. How have you defined all sales strategy requirements first?
<--- Score

87. Is scope creep really all bad news?
<--- Score

88. What sources do you use to gather information for a sales strategy study?
<--- Score

89. Why are you doing sales strategy and what is the scope?
<--- Score

90. How do you build the right business case?

<--- Score

91. What are the sales strategy tasks and definitions?
<--- Score

92. Are task requirements clearly defined?
<--- Score

93. In what way can you redefine the criteria of choice clients have in your category in your favor?
<--- Score

94. Where can you gather more information?
<--- Score

95. Is there a completed, verified, and validated high-level 'as is' (not 'should be' or 'could be') stakeholder process map?
<--- Score

96. Is there a sales strategy management charter, including stakeholder case, problem and goal statements, scope, milestones, roles and responsibilities, communication plan?
<--- Score

97. What information should you gather?
<--- Score

98. Are all requirements met?
<--- Score

99. What happens if sales strategy's scope changes?
<--- Score

100. Are required metrics defined, what are they?

<--- Score

101. What is the scope of sales strategy?
<--- Score

102. What are the sales strategy use cases?
<--- Score

103. Is the scope of sales strategy defined?
<--- Score

104. Has your scope been defined?
<--- Score

105. How did the sales strategy manager receive input to the development of a sales strategy improvement plan and the estimated completion dates/times of each activity?
<--- Score

106. Is the work to date meeting requirements?
<--- Score

107. What intelligence can you gather?
<--- Score

108. What are (control) requirements for sales strategy Information?
<--- Score

109. How can the value of sales strategy be defined?
<--- Score

110. How do you keep key subject matter experts in the loop?
<--- Score

111. What would be the goal or target for a sales strategy's improvement team?
<--- Score

112. How would you define sales strategy leadership?
<--- Score

113. Is the team formed and are team leaders (Coaches and Management Leads) assigned?
<--- Score

114. Has/have the customer(s) been identified?
<--- Score

115. Is the sales strategy scope complete and appropriately sized?
<--- Score

116. What are the rough order estimates on cost savings/opportunities that sales strategy brings?
<--- Score

117. Has anyone else (internal or external to the group) attempted to solve this problem or a similar one before? If so, what knowledge can be leveraged from these previous efforts?
<--- Score

118. Are different versions of process maps needed to account for the different types of inputs?
<--- Score

119. What is out of scope?
<--- Score

120. Is special sales strategy user knowledge required?
<--- Score

121. Is it clearly defined in and to your organization what you do?
<--- Score

122. Who is gathering information?
<--- Score

123. What was the context?
<--- Score

124. Will team members regularly document their sales strategy work?
<--- Score

125. Does the scope remain the same?
<--- Score

126. Is the sales strategy scope manageable?
<--- Score

127. What system do you use for gathering sales strategy information?
<--- Score

128. Are the sales strategy requirements complete?
<--- Score

129. What constraints exist that might impact the team?
<--- Score

130. Are customer(s) identified and segmented according to their different needs and requirements?

<--- Score

131. Has a project plan, Gantt chart, or similar been developed/completed?
<--- Score

132. How do you gather sales strategy requirements?
<--- Score

133. The political context: who holds power?
<--- Score

134. Has the direction changed at all during the course of sales strategy? If so, when did it change and why?
<--- Score

135. Has a team charter been developed and communicated?
<--- Score

136. Are there different segments of customers?
<--- Score

137. What is in scope?
<--- Score

138. Is sales strategy required?
<--- Score

139. How was the 'as is' process map developed, reviewed, verified and validated?
<--- Score

140. Is the improvement team aware of the different versions of a process: what they think it is vs. what it

actually is vs. what it should be vs. what it could be?
<--- Score

141. How will variation in the actual durations of each activity be dealt with to ensure that the expected sales strategy results are met?
<--- Score

142. Is full participation by members in regularly held team meetings guaranteed?
<--- Score

Add up total points for this section:
_ _ _ _ _ = Total points for this section

Divided by: _ _ _ _ _ _ (number of statements answered) = _ _ _ _ _ _
Average score for this section

Transfer your score to the sales strategy Index at the beginning of the Self-Assessment.

CRITERION #3: MEASURE:

INTENT: Gather the correct data.
Measure the current performance and
evolution of the situation.

In my belief, the answer to this
question is clearly defined:

5 Strongly Agree

4 Agree

3 Neutral

2 Disagree

1 Strongly Disagree

1. Will sales strategy have an impact on current
business continuity, disaster recovery processes and/
or infrastructure?
<--- Score

2. What is an unallowable cost?
<--- Score

3. Why do you expend time and effort to implement

measurement, for whom?
<--- Score

4. How is the value delivered by sales strategy being measured?
<--- Score

5. How can you measure sales strategy in a systematic way?
<--- Score

6. Are there any easy-to-implement alternatives to sales strategy? Sometimes other solutions are available that do not require the cost implications of a full-blown project?
<--- Score

7. What causes extra work or rework?
<--- Score

8. What does verifying compliance entail?
<--- Score

9. How to cause the change?
<--- Score

10. Does a sales strategy quantification method exist?
<--- Score

11. At what cost?
<--- Score

12. How do you verify performance?
<--- Score

13. What does losing customers cost your

organization?
<--- Score

14. How can a sales strategy test verify your ideas or assumptions?
<--- Score

15. What measurements are being captured?
<--- Score

16. What details are required of the sales strategy cost structure?
<--- Score

17. How will you measure success?
<--- Score

18. How do you verify the sales strategy requirements quality?
<--- Score

19. How do you measure success?
<--- Score

20. What would be a real cause for concern?
<--- Score

21. What users will be impacted?
<--- Score

22. Do you verify that corrective actions were taken?
<--- Score

23. How do you prevent mis-estimating cost?
<--- Score

24. What are hidden sales strategy quality costs?
<--- Score

25. What drives O&M cost?
<--- Score

26. Where is it measured?
<--- Score

27. Which costs should be taken into account?
<--- Score

28. How can you reduce the costs of obtaining inputs?
<--- Score

29. What causes innovation to fail or succeed in your organization?
<--- Score

30. Do the benefits outweigh the costs?
<--- Score

31. What is the cost of rework?
<--- Score

32. What is measured? Why?
<--- Score

33. What relevant entities could be measured?
<--- Score

34. How do you measure lifecycle phases?
<--- Score

35. What can be used to verify compliance?
<--- Score

36. What potential environmental factors impact the sales strategy effort?
<--- Score

37. How will measures be used to manage and adapt?
<--- Score

38. Do you have an issue in getting priority?
<--- Score

39. Are there competing sales strategy priorities?
<--- Score

40. Is there an opportunity to verify requirements?
<--- Score

41. What tests verify requirements?
<--- Score

42. How do your measurements capture actionable sales strategy information for use in exceeding your customers expectations and securing your customers engagement?
<--- Score

43. What are the strategic priorities for this year?
<--- Score

44. How do you quantify and qualify impacts?
<--- Score

45. When are costs are incurred?
<--- Score

46. Does management have the right priorities

among projects?
<--- Score

47. Do you effectively measure and reward individual and team performance?
<--- Score

48. Are supply costs steady or fluctuating?
<--- Score

49. Do you have a flow diagram of what happens?
<--- Score

50. How sensitive must the sales strategy strategy be to cost?
<--- Score

51. What are the operational costs after sales strategy deployment?
<--- Score

52. What are the current costs of the sales strategy process?
<--- Score

53. How will success or failure be measured?
<--- Score

54. Is the solution cost-effective?
<--- Score

55. Are sales strategy vulnerabilities categorized and prioritized?
<--- Score

56. Where can you go to verify the info?

<--- Score

57. How can you measure the performance?
<--- Score

58. How do you control the overall costs of your work processes?
<--- Score

59. What happens if cost savings do not materialize?
<--- Score

60. Have you made assumptions about the shape of the future, particularly its impact on your customers and competitors?
<--- Score

61. Are the units of measure consistent?
<--- Score

62. What causes mismanagement?
<--- Score

63. How do you verify the authenticity of the data and information used?
<--- Score

64. When a disaster occurs, who gets priority?
<--- Score

65. What are your customers expectations and measures?
<--- Score

66. Have you included everything in your sales strategy cost models?

<--- Score

67. What do people want to verify?
<--- Score

68. Are the measurements objective?
<--- Score

69. What disadvantage does this cause for the user?
<--- Score

70. What are you verifying?
<--- Score

71. Is it possible to estimate the impact of unanticipated complexity such as wrong or failed assumptions, feedback, etcetera on proposed reforms?
<--- Score

72. What could cause you to change course?
<--- Score

73. What are allowable costs?
<--- Score

74. What evidence is there and what is measured?
<--- Score

75. How will your organization measure success?
<--- Score

76. What is the root cause(s) of the problem?
<--- Score

77. Was a business case (cost/benefit) developed?

<--- Score

78. Are the sales strategy benefits worth its costs?
<--- Score

79. Where is the cost?
<--- Score

80. Does the sales strategy task fit the client's priorities?
<--- Score

81. What are the sales strategy key cost drivers?
<--- Score

82. Are you taking your company in the direction of better and revenue or cheaper and cost?
<--- Score

83. Are actual costs in line with budgeted costs?
<--- Score

84. What causes investor action?
<--- Score

85. Do you have any cost sales strategy limitation requirements?
<--- Score

86. What measurements are possible, practicable and meaningful?
<--- Score

87. When should you bother with diagrams?
<--- Score

88. What are your operating costs?
<--- Score

89. How will you measure your sales strategy effectiveness?
<--- Score

90. What are the costs of delaying sales strategy action?
<--- Score

91. What are your primary costs, revenues, assets?
<--- Score

92. What methods are feasible and acceptable to estimate the impact of reforms?
<--- Score

93. How do you measure efficient delivery of sales strategy services?
<--- Score

94. Did you tackle the cause or the symptom?
<--- Score

95. What is the total cost related to deploying sales strategy, including any consulting or professional services?
<--- Score

96. What are the estimated costs of proposed changes?
<--- Score

97. What is the cause of any sales strategy gaps?
<--- Score

98. How do you verify and validate the sales strategy data?
<--- Score

99. How do you measure variability?
<--- Score

100. What is your sales strategy quality cost segregation study?
<--- Score

101. Among the sales strategy product and service cost to be estimated, which is considered hardest to estimate?
<--- Score

102. What does a Test Case verify?
<--- Score

103. How can you reduce costs?
<--- Score

104. What are the uncertainties surrounding estimates of impact?
<--- Score

105. How long to keep data and how to manage retention costs?
<--- Score

106. How do you verify and develop ideas and innovations?
<--- Score

107. How is progress measured?

<--- Score

108. Are indirect costs charged to the sales strategy program?
<--- Score

109. Who pays the cost?
<--- Score

110. How are measurements made?
<--- Score

111. How do you verify if sales strategy is built right?
<--- Score

112. How can you manage cost down?
<--- Score

113. How are costs allocated?
<--- Score

114. Are there measurements based on task performance?
<--- Score

115. Has a cost center been established?
<--- Score

116. Are you aware of what could cause a problem?
<--- Score

117. What are your key sales strategy organizational performance measures, including key short and longer-term financial measures?
<--- Score

118. Who is involved in verifying compliance?
<--- Score

119. How frequently do you track sales strategy measures?
<--- Score

120. What are the sales strategy investment costs?
<--- Score

121. How do you aggregate measures across priorities?
<--- Score

122. What is the total fixed cost?
<--- Score

123. How will effects be measured?
<--- Score

124. What are the costs?
<--- Score

125. Which measures and indicators matter?
<--- Score

126. What is the sales strategy business impact?
<--- Score

127. Do you aggressively reward and promote the people who have the biggest impact on creating excellent sales strategy services/products?
<--- Score

128. Have design-to-cost goals been established?
<--- Score

129. How do you verify your resources?
<--- Score

130. What do you measure and why?
<--- Score

131. Which sales strategy impacts are significant?
<--- Score

132. Why do the measurements/indicators matter?
<--- Score

133. What are the costs and benefits?
<--- Score

134. What would it cost to replace your technology?
<--- Score

135. Who should receive measurement reports?
<--- Score

136. What is your decision requirements diagram?
<--- Score

137. Are you able to realize any cost savings?
<--- Score

138. What harm might be caused?
<--- Score

Add up total points for this section:
_ _ _ _ _ = Total points for this section

Divided by: _ _ _ _ _ _ (number of
statements answered) = _ _ _ _ _ _

Average score for this section

Transfer your score to the sales strategy Index at the beginning of the Self-Assessment.

CRITERION #4: ANALYZE:

INTENT: Analyze causes, assumptions and hypotheses.

In my belief, the answer to this question is clearly defined:

5 Strongly Agree

4 Agree

3 Neutral

2 Disagree

1 Strongly Disagree

1. Where is the data coming from to measure compliance?
<--- Score

2. Is there an established change management process?
<--- Score

3. What are the necessary qualifications?
<--- Score

4. Was a detailed process map created to amplify critical steps of the 'as is' stakeholder process?
<--- Score

5. What sales strategy data should be managed?
<--- Score

6. What sales strategy metrics are outputs of the process?
<--- Score

7. Has an output goal been set?
<--- Score

8. Who is involved with workflow mapping?
<--- Score

9. Where is sales strategy data gathered?
<--- Score

10. What are your current levels and trends in key measures or indicators of sales strategy product and process performance that are important to and directly serve your customers? How do these results compare with the performance of your competitors and other organizations with similar offerings?
<--- Score

11. What were the financial benefits resulting from any 'ground fruit or low-hanging fruit' (quick fixes)?
<--- Score

12. Who is involved in the management review process?
<--- Score

13. Do quality systems drive continuous improvement?
<--- Score

14. Is the suppliers process defined and controlled?
<--- Score

15. What are the best opportunities for value improvement?
<--- Score

16. What are your outputs?
<--- Score

17. Did any additional data need to be collected?
<--- Score

18. What successful thing are you doing today that may be blinding you to new growth opportunities?
<--- Score

19. What tools were used to generate the list of possible causes?
<--- Score

20. What information qualified as important?
<--- Score

21. What is the oversight process?
<--- Score

22. How do you measure the operational performance of your key work systems and processes, including productivity, cycle time, and other appropriate measures of process effectiveness, efficiency, and

innovation?

<--- Score

23. What systems/processes must you excel at?

<--- Score

24. How is the data gathered?

<--- Score

25. How do you define collaboration and team output?

<--- Score

26. Is the gap/opportunity displayed and communicated in financial terms?

<--- Score

27. What data is gathered?

<--- Score

28. Is pre-qualification of suppliers carried out?

<--- Score

29. Record-keeping requirements flow from the records needed as inputs, outputs, controls and for transformation of a sales strategy process, are the records needed as inputs to the sales strategy process available?

<--- Score

30. Are all team members qualified for all tasks?

<--- Score

31. Can you add value to the current sales strategy decision-making process (largely qualitative) by incorporating uncertainty modeling (more

quantitative)?
<--- Score

32. Do you have the authority to produce the output?
<--- Score

33. What are your current levels and trends in key
sales strategy measures or indicators of product
and process performance that are important to and
directly serve your customers?
<--- Score

34. How is sales strategy data gathered?
<--- Score

35. How do you ensure that the sales strategy
opportunity is realistic?
<--- Score

36. What sales strategy data should be collected?
<--- Score

37. What quality tools were used to get through the
analyze phase?
<--- Score

38. Were there any improvement opportunities
identified from the process analysis?
<--- Score

39. Have you defined which data is gathered how?
<--- Score

40. Were Pareto charts (or similar) used to portray the
'heavy hitters' (or key sources of variation)?
<--- Score

41. Have any additional benefits been identified that will result from closing all or most of the gaps?
<--- Score

42. What are your sales strategy processes?
<--- Score

43. Is the sales strategy process severely broken such that a re-design is necessary?
<--- Score

44. How do you implement and manage your work processes to ensure that they meet design requirements?
<--- Score

45. How does the organization define, manage, and improve its sales strategy processes?
<--- Score

46. How will the data be checked for quality?
<--- Score

47. Do your contracts/agreements contain data security obligations?
<--- Score

48. How are outputs preserved and protected?
<--- Score

49. What is your organizations process which leads to recognition of value generation?
<--- Score

50. What are your best practices for minimizing sales

strategy project risk, while demonstrating incremental value and quick wins throughout the sales strategy project lifecycle?

<--- Score

51. What types of data do your sales strategy indicators require?

<--- Score

52. How is the way you as the leader think and process information affecting your organizational culture?

<--- Score

53. How do you use sales strategy data and information to support organizational decision making and innovation?

<--- Score

54. Is the required sales strategy data gathered?

<--- Score

55. How is data used for program management and improvement?

<--- Score

56. What is the Value Stream Mapping?

<--- Score

57. What training and qualifications will you need?

<--- Score

58. Was a cause-and-effect diagram used to explore the different types of causes (or sources of variation)?

<--- Score

59. What is the sales strategy Driver?

<--- Score

60. What is the complexity of the output produced?
<--- Score

61. What sales strategy data will be collected?
<--- Score

62. How was the detailed process map generated, verified, and validated?
<--- Score

63. What are the sales strategy business drivers?
<--- Score

64. How is the sales strategy Value Stream Mapping managed?
<--- Score

65. Are your outputs consistent?
<--- Score

66. What were the crucial 'moments of truth' on the process map?
<--- Score

67. What, related to, sales strategy processes does your organization outsource?
<--- Score

68. Who owns what data?
<--- Score

69. When should a process be art not science?
<--- Score

70. What is your organizations system for selecting qualified vendors?
<--- Score

71. What other organizational variables, such as reward systems or communication systems, affect the performance of this sales strategy process?
<--- Score

72. What qualifies as competition?
<--- Score

73. How do your work systems and key work processes relate to and capitalize on your core competencies?
<--- Score

74. What qualifications do sales strategy leaders need?
<--- Score

75. Is there any way to speed up the process?
<--- Score

76. How has the sales strategy data been gathered?
<--- Score

77. Think about some of the processes you undertake within your organization, which do you own?
<--- Score

78. Do several people in different organizational units assist with the sales strategy process?
<--- Score

79. How many input/output points does it require?
<--- Score

80. What are the sales strategy design outputs?
<--- Score

81. What internal processes need improvement?
<--- Score

82. What other jobs or tasks affect the performance of the steps in the sales strategy process?
<--- Score

83. Think about the functions involved in your sales strategy project, what processes flow from these functions?
<--- Score

84. What are evaluation criteria for the output?
<--- Score

85. What is the output?
<--- Score

86. What qualifications are needed?
<--- Score

87. What are the revised rough estimates of the financial savings/opportunity for sales strategy improvements?
<--- Score

88. What sales strategy data do you gather or use now?
<--- Score

89. What qualifications and skills do you need?
<--- Score

90. What methods do you use to gather sales strategy data?
<--- Score

91. A compounding model resolution with available relevant data can often provide insight towards a solution methodology; which sales strategy models, tools and techniques are necessary?
<--- Score

92. Who will gather what data?
<--- Score

93. How difficult is it to qualify what sales strategy ROI is?
<--- Score

94. What controls do you have in place to protect data?
<--- Score

95. Who will facilitate the team and process?
<--- Score

96. Did any value-added analysis or 'lean thinking' take place to identify some of the gaps shown on the 'as is' process map?
<--- Score

97. What data do you need to collect?
<--- Score

98. What is the cost of poor quality as supported by the team's analysis?
<--- Score

99. Are gaps between current performance and the goal performance identified?
<--- Score

100. Where can you get qualified talent today?
<--- Score

101. What process improvements will be needed?
<--- Score

102. Is data and process analysis, root cause analysis and quantifying the gap/opportunity in place?
<--- Score

103. What does the data say about the performance of the stakeholder process?
<--- Score

104. What qualifications are necessary?
<--- Score

105. What do you need to qualify?
<--- Score

106. An organizationally feasible system request is one that considers the mission, goals and objectives of the organization, key questions are: is the sales strategy solution request practical and will it solve a problem or take advantage of an opportunity to achieve company goals?
<--- Score

107. What conclusions were drawn from the team's data collection and analysis? How did the team reach these conclusions?

<--- Score

108. How much data can be collected in the given timeframe?
<--- Score

109. Is the final output clearly identified?
<--- Score

110. What are your key performance measures or indicators and in-process measures for the control and improvement of your sales strategy processes?
<--- Score

111. What output to create?
<--- Score

112. Who qualifies to gain access to data?
<--- Score

113. How do mission and objectives affect the sales strategy processes of your organization?
<--- Score

114. What are the disruptive sales strategy technologies that enable your organization to radically change your business processes?
<--- Score

115. Have the problem and goal statements been updated to reflect the additional knowledge gained from the analyze phase?
<--- Score

116. How will the change process be managed?
<--- Score

117. How will the sales strategy data be captured?
<--- Score

118. Do staff qualifications match your project?
<--- Score

119. Who gets your output?
<--- Score

120. What process should you select for improvement?
<--- Score

121. How do you identify specific sales strategy investment opportunities and emerging trends?
<--- Score

122. Is the performance gap determined?
<--- Score

123. Do you, as a leader, bounce back quickly from setbacks?
<--- Score

124. What kind of crime could a potential new hire have committed that would not only not disqualify him/her from being hired by your organization, but would actually indicate that he/she might be a particularly good fit?
<--- Score

125. Were any designed experiments used to generate additional insight into the data analysis?
<--- Score

126. Do your employees have the opportunity to do what they do best everyday?
<--- Score

127. What did the team gain from developing a sub-process map?
<--- Score

128. What are the processes for audit reporting and management?
<--- Score

129. Is there a strict change management process?
<--- Score

130. Should you invest in industry-recognized qualifications?
<--- Score

131. How often will data be collected for measures?
<--- Score

132. Which sales strategy data should be retained?
<--- Score

133. How will corresponding data be collected?
<--- Score

134. Are you missing sales strategy opportunities?
<--- Score

135. Are sales strategy changes recognized early enough to be approved through the regular process?
<--- Score

136. What tools were used to narrow the list of

possible causes?
<--- Score

137. Do you understand your management processes today?
<--- Score

Add up total points for this section:
_ _ _ _ _ = Total points for this section

Divided by: _ _ _ _ _ _ (number of statements answered) = _ _ _ _ _ _
Average score for this section

Transfer your score to the sales strategy Index at the beginning of the Self-Assessment.

CRITERION #5: IMPROVE:

INTENT: Develop a practical solution. Innovate, establish and test the solution and to measure the results.

In my belief, the answer to this question is clearly defined:

5 Strongly Agree

4 Agree

3 Neutral

2 Disagree

1 Strongly Disagree

1. How will you recognize and celebrate results?
<--- Score

2. Does a good decision guarantee a good outcome?
<--- Score

3. How do you keep improving sales strategy?
<--- Score

4. Who will be responsible for documenting the sales strategy requirements in detail?
<--- Score

5. How do the sales strategy results compare with the performance of your competitors and other organizations with similar offerings?
<--- Score

6. Can you integrate quality management and risk management?
<--- Score

7. Do you need to do a usability evaluation?
<--- Score

8. What lessons, if any, from a pilot were incorporated into the design of the full-scale solution?
<--- Score

9. For estimation problems, how do you develop an estimation statement?
<--- Score

10. How can the phases of sales strategy development be identified?
<--- Score

11. Are risk management tasks balanced centrally and locally?
<--- Score

12. Do you combine technical expertise with business knowledge and sales strategy Key topics include lifecycles, development approaches, requirements and how to make a business case?

<--- Score

13. Are the most efficient solutions problem-specific?
<--- Score

14. Do those selected for the sales strategy team have a good general understanding of what sales strategy is all about?
<--- Score

15. Who are the people involved in developing and implementing sales strategy?
<--- Score

16. Who manages supplier risk management in your organization?
<--- Score

17. Where do you need sales strategy improvement?
<--- Score

18. What are the expected sales strategy results?
<--- Score

19. What went well, what should change, what can improve?
<--- Score

20. Have you achieved sales strategy improvements?
<--- Score

21. If you could go back in time five years, what decision would you make differently? What is your best guess as to what decision you're making today you might regret five years from now?
<--- Score

22. What are the implications of the one critical sales strategy decision 10 minutes, 10 months, and 10 years from now?
<--- Score

23. How do you improve your likelihood of success ?
<--- Score

24. Who do you report sales strategy results to?
<--- Score

25. What is the magnitude of the improvements?
<--- Score

26. Is the measure of success for sales strategy understandable to a variety of people?
<--- Score

27. How are policy decisions made and where?
<--- Score

28. Is the sales strategy solution sustainable?
<--- Score

29. Are the risks fully understood, reasonable and manageable?
<--- Score

30. Does the goal represent a desired result that can be measured?
<--- Score

31. What criteria will you use to assess your sales strategy risks?
<--- Score

32. Are procedures documented for managing sales strategy risks?
<--- Score

33. How does the team improve its work?
<--- Score

34. Are you assessing sales strategy and risk?
<--- Score

35. Do you cover the five essential competencies: Communication, Collaboration,Innovation, Adaptability, and Leadership that improve an organizations ability to leverage the new sales strategy in a volatile global economy?
<--- Score

36. How do you manage sales strategy risk?
<--- Score

37. Do vendor agreements bring new compliance risk ?
<--- Score

38. Are events managed to resolution?
<--- Score

39. What error proofing will be done to address some of the discrepancies observed in the 'as is' process?
<--- Score

40. What improvements have been achieved?
<--- Score

41. What alternative responses are available to

manage risk?

<--- Score

42. How can skill-level changes improve sales strategy?

<--- Score

43. Who controls the risk?

<--- Score

44. When you map the key players in your own work and the types/domains of relationships with them, which relationships do you find easy and which challenging, and why?

<--- Score

45. What is sales strategy risk?

<--- Score

46. How do you measure improved sales strategy service perception, and satisfaction?

<--- Score

47. Can you identify any significant risks or exposures to sales strategy third- parties (vendors, service providers, alliance partners etc) that concern you?

<--- Score

48. What tools were used to tap into the creativity and encourage 'outside the box' thinking?

<--- Score

49. Is any sales strategy documentation required?

<--- Score

50. What are the sales strategy security risks?

<--- Score

51. How does your organization evaluate strategic sales strategy success?
<--- Score

52. What sales strategy improvements can be made?
<--- Score

53. Is there any other sales strategy solution?
<--- Score

54. Explorations of the frontiers of sales strategy will help you build influence, improve sales strategy, optimize decision making, and sustain change, what is your approach?
<--- Score

55. What strategies for sales strategy improvement are successful?
<--- Score

56. What communications are necessary to support the implementation of the solution?
<--- Score

57. What resources are required for the improvement efforts?
<--- Score

58. Who are the sales strategy decision makers?
<--- Score

59. What are the concrete sales strategy results?
<--- Score

60. How do you go about comparing sales strategy approaches/solutions?
<--- Score

61. Is there a small-scale pilot for proposed improvement(s)? What conclusions were drawn from the outcomes of a pilot?
<--- Score

62. In the past few months, what is the smallest change you have made that has had the biggest positive result? What was it about that small change that produced the large return?
<--- Score

63. How is knowledge sharing about risk management improved?
<--- Score

64. What risks do you need to manage?
<--- Score

65. What current systems have to be understood and/ or changed?
<--- Score

66. Were any criteria developed to assist the team in testing and evaluating potential solutions?
<--- Score

67. Is sales strategy documentation maintained?
<--- Score

68. sales strategy risk decisions: whose call Is It?
<--- Score

69. What assumptions are made about the solution and approach?
<--- Score

70. How do you measure progress and evaluate training effectiveness?
<--- Score

71. What tools do you use once you have decided on a sales strategy strategy and more importantly how do you choose?
<--- Score

72. Would you develop a sales strategy Communication Strategy?
<--- Score

73. What were the criteria for evaluating a sales strategy pilot?
<--- Score

74. What should a proof of concept or pilot accomplish?
<--- Score

75. What attendant changes will need to be made to ensure that the solution is successful?
<--- Score

76. Who controls key decisions that will be made?
<--- Score

77. What does the 'should be' process map/design look like?
<--- Score

78. Risk Identification: What are the possible risk events your organization faces in relation to sales strategy?
<--- Score

79. Are risk triggers captured?
<--- Score

80. Where do the sales strategy decisions reside?
<--- Score

81. How do you improve sales strategy service perception, and satisfaction?
<--- Score

82. Which of the recognised risks out of all risks can be most likely transferred?
<--- Score

83. Who should make the sales strategy decisions?
<--- Score

84. To what extent does management recognize sales strategy as a tool to increase the results?
<--- Score

85. How will you know that you have improved?
<--- Score

86. What is the implementation plan?
<--- Score

87. How significant is the improvement in the eyes of the end user?
<--- Score

88. Is the sales strategy documentation thorough?
<--- Score

89. What actually has to improve and by how much?
<--- Score

90. Is the solution technically practical?
<--- Score

91. Was a pilot designed for the proposed solution(s)?
<--- Score

92. Who are the key stakeholders for the sales strategy evaluation?
<--- Score

93. What tools were used to evaluate the potential solutions?
<--- Score

94. How do you link measurement and risk?
<--- Score

95. For decision problems, how do you develop a decision statement?
<--- Score

96. Is supporting sales strategy documentation required?
<--- Score

97. Is there a high likelihood that any recommendations will achieve their intended results?
<--- Score

98. Is there a cost/benefit analysis of optimal

solution(s)?
<--- Score

99. Which sales strategy solution is appropriate?
<--- Score

100. Who will be responsible for making the decisions to include or exclude requested changes once sales strategy is underway?
<--- Score

101. What do you want to improve?
<--- Score

102. How risky is your organization?
<--- Score

103. Do you have the optimal project management team structure?
<--- Score

104. What area needs the greatest improvement?
<--- Score

105. How can you better manage risk?
<--- Score

106. How scalable is your sales strategy solution?
<--- Score

107. How do you decide how much to remunerate an employee?
<--- Score

108. Are decisions made in a timely manner?
<--- Score

109. What were the underlying assumptions on the cost-benefit analysis?
<--- Score

110. How do you define the solutions' scope?
<--- Score

111. What is the team's contingency plan for potential problems occurring in implementation?
<--- Score

112. What needs improvement? Why?
<--- Score

113. Can the solution be designed and implemented within an acceptable time period?
<--- Score

114. How is continuous improvement applied to risk management?
<--- Score

115. How do you mitigate sales strategy risk?
<--- Score

116. How will you know that a change is an improvement?
<--- Score

117. Why improve in the first place?
<--- Score

118. What to do with the results or outcomes of measurements?
<--- Score

119. Is risk periodically assessed?
<--- Score

120. Is the scope clearly documented?
<--- Score

121. Who are the sales strategy decision-makers?
<--- Score

122. What is sales strategy's impact on utilizing the best solution(s)?
<--- Score

123. How do you improve productivity?
<--- Score

124. At what point will vulnerability assessments be performed once sales strategy is put into production (e.g., ongoing Risk Management after implementation)?
<--- Score

125. How will you know when its improved?
<--- Score

126. What are the affordable sales strategy risks?
<--- Score

127. How can you improve sales strategy?
<--- Score

128. Is the sales strategy risk managed?
<--- Score

129. Risk factors: what are the characteristics of sales

strategy that make it risky?

<--- Score

130. What practices helps your organization to develop its capacity to recognize patterns?

<--- Score

131. Is the optimal solution selected based on testing and analysis?

<--- Score

132. How do you measure risk?

<--- Score

133. How are sales strategy risks managed?

<--- Score

134. How do you deal with sales strategy risk?

<--- Score

135. Who makes the sales strategy decisions in your organization?

<--- Score

136. How do you manage and improve your sales strategy work systems to deliver customer value and achieve organizational success and sustainability?

<--- Score

137. What is the sales strategy's sustainability risk?

<--- Score

138. What tools were most useful during the improve phase?

<--- Score

139. Are the key business and technology risks being managed?
<--- Score

Add up total points for this section:
_ _ _ _ _ = Total points for this section

Divided by: _ _ _ _ _ _ (number of
statements answered) = _ _ _ _ _ _
Average score for this section

Transfer your score to the sales strategy
Index at the beginning of the Self-
Assessment.

CRITERION #6: CONTROL:

INTENT: Implement the practical solution. Maintain the performance and correct possible complications.

In my belief, the answer to this question is clearly defined:

5 Strongly Agree

4 Agree

3 Neutral

2 Disagree

1 Strongly Disagree

1. Are new process steps, standards, and documentation ingrained into normal operations?
<--- Score

2. How do your controls stack up?
<--- Score

3. Are operating procedures consistent?
<--- Score

4. How is sales strategy project cost planned, managed, monitored?
<--- Score

5. Are controls in place and consistently applied?
<--- Score

6. Do the viable solutions scale to future needs?
<--- Score

7. What quality tools were useful in the control phase?
<--- Score

8. How might the group capture best practices and lessons learned so as to leverage improvements?
<--- Score

9. What do your reports reflect?
<--- Score

10. What do you stand for--and what are you against?
<--- Score

11. How will the day-to-day responsibilities for monitoring and continual improvement be transferred from the improvement team to the process owner?
<--- Score

12. What is the recommended frequency of auditing?
<--- Score

13. Does your sales strategy reflect a change in buyer behavior?
<--- Score

14. Is there an action plan in case of emergencies?
<--- Score

15. Will the team be available to assist members in planning investigations?
<--- Score

16. How do you encourage people to take control and responsibility?
<--- Score

17. You may have created your quality measures at a time when you lacked resources, technology wasn't up to the required standard, or low service levels were the industry norm. Have those circumstances changed?
<--- Score

18. What are customers monitoring?
<--- Score

19. Are suggested corrective/restorative actions indicated on the response plan for known causes to problems that might surface?
<--- Score

20. Who sets the sales strategy standards?
<--- Score

21. Is there a control plan in place for sustaining improvements (short and long-term)?
<--- Score

22. Are documented procedures clear and easy to follow for the operators?

<--- Score

23. Has the sales strategy value of standards been quantified?
<--- Score

24. How do senior leaders actions reflect a commitment to the organizations sales strategy values?
<--- Score

25. Are pertinent alerts monitored, analyzed and distributed to appropriate personnel?
<--- Score

26. Are the sales strategy standards challenging?
<--- Score

27. Do the sales strategy decisions you make today help people and the planet tomorrow?
<--- Score

28. Are there documented procedures?
<--- Score

29. Is there a recommended audit plan for routine surveillance inspections of sales strategy's gains?
<--- Score

30. Is new knowledge gained imbedded in the response plan?
<--- Score

31. Is the sales strategy test/monitoring cost justified?
<--- Score

32. How widespread is its use?
<--- Score

33. How likely is the current sales strategy plan to come in on schedule or on budget?
<--- Score

34. What are the critical parameters to watch?
<--- Score

35. Is there documentation that will support the successful operation of the improvement?
<--- Score

36. How do you select, collect, align, and integrate sales strategy data and information for tracking daily operations and overall organizational performance, including progress relative to strategic objectives and action plans?
<--- Score

37. How will input, process, and output variables be checked to detect for sub-optimal conditions?
<--- Score

38. Are the planned controls in place?
<--- Score

39. Is there a transfer of ownership and knowledge to process owner and process team tasked with the responsibilities.
<--- Score

40. What is the best design framework for sales strategy organization now that, in a post industrial-age if the top-down, command and control model is

no longer relevant?
<--- Score

41. How do you spread information?
<--- Score

42. What key inputs and outputs are being measured
on an ongoing basis?
<--- Score

43. What are the key elements of your sales strategy
performance improvement system, including your
evaluation, organizational learning, and innovation
processes?
<--- Score

44. Does a troubleshooting guide exist or is it needed?
<--- Score

45. Against what alternative is success being
measured?
<--- Score

46. What should you measure to verify efficiency
gains?
<--- Score

47. Act/Adjust: What Do you Need to Do Differently?
<--- Score

48. What are the performance and scale of the sales
strategy tools?
<--- Score

49. Where do ideas that reach policy makers and
planners as proposals for sales strategy strengthening

and reform actually originate?
<--- Score

50. How is change control managed?
<--- Score

51. What are your results for key measures or
indicators of the accomplishment of your sales
strategy strategy and action plans, including building
and strengthening core competencies?
<--- Score

52. Will existing staff require re-training, for example,
to learn new business processes?
<--- Score

53. Is there a standardized process?
<--- Score

54. Will your goals reflect your program budget?
<--- Score

55. What is the control/monitoring plan?
<--- Score

56. What other areas of the group might benefit from
the sales strategy team's improvements, knowledge,
and learning?
<--- Score

57. Is there a sales strategy Communication plan
covering who needs to get what information when?
<--- Score

58. Has the improved process and its steps been
standardized?

<--- Score

59. Can support from partners be adjusted?
<--- Score

60. How will report readings be checked to effectively monitor performance?
<--- Score

61. How will sales strategy decisions be made and monitored?
<--- Score

62. How will new or emerging customer needs/ requirements be checked/communicated to orient the process toward meeting the new specifications and continually reducing variation?
<--- Score

63. Is reporting being used or needed?
<--- Score

64. Have new or revised work instructions resulted?
<--- Score

65. Is knowledge gained on process shared and institutionalized?
<--- Score

66. What are you attempting to measure/monitor?
<--- Score

67. How do controls support value?
<--- Score

68. Who will be in control?

<--- Score

69. How do you plan for the cost of succession?
<--- Score

70. Is there a documented and implemented monitoring plan?
<--- Score

71. Can you adapt and adjust to changing sales strategy situations?
<--- Score

72. Who controls critical resources?
<--- Score

73. Does the sales strategy performance meet the customer's requirements?
<--- Score

74. Who is going to spread your message?
<--- Score

75. What is the standard for acceptable sales strategy performance?
<--- Score

76. How do you plan on providing proper recognition and disclosure of supporting companies?
<--- Score

77. What do you measure to verify effectiveness gains?
<--- Score

78. Is a response plan established and deployed?

<--- Score

79. How will the process owner and team be able to hold the gains?
<--- Score

80. Is a response plan in place for when the input, process, or output measures indicate an 'out-of-control' condition?
<--- Score

81. What should the next improvement project be that is related to sales strategy?
<--- Score

82. In the case of a sales strategy project, the criteria for the audit derive from implementation objectives, an audit of a sales strategy project involves assessing whether the recommendations outlined for implementation have been met, can you track that any sales strategy project is implemented as planned, and is it working?
<--- Score

83. How will the process owner verify improvement in present and future sigma levels, process capabilities?
<--- Score

84. Does sales strategy appropriately measure and monitor risk?
<--- Score

85. What sales strategy standards are applicable?
<--- Score

86. What adjustments to the strategies are needed?

<--- Score

87. Do you monitor the effectiveness of your sales strategy activities?
<--- Score

88. Who has control over resources?
<--- Score

89. How do you monitor usage and cost?
<--- Score

90. Does the response plan contain a definite closed loop continual improvement scheme (e.g., plan-do-check-act)?
<--- Score

91. Who is the sales strategy process owner?
<--- Score

92. Will any special training be provided for results interpretation?
<--- Score

93. How can you best use all of your knowledge repositories to enhance learning and sharing?
<--- Score

94. Do you monitor the sales strategy decisions made and fine tune them as they evolve?
<--- Score

95. What other systems, operations, processes, and infrastructures (hiring practices, staffing, training, incentives/rewards, metrics/dashboards/scorecards, etc.) need updates, additions, changes, or deletions

in order to facilitate knowledge transfer and improvements?
<--- Score

96. What is your theory of human motivation, and how does your compensation plan fit with that view?
<--- Score

97. Does job training on the documented procedures need to be part of the process team's education and training?
<--- Score

98. How do you establish and deploy modified action plans if circumstances require a shift in plans and rapid execution of new plans?
<--- Score

99. What are the known security controls?
<--- Score

100. How will you measure your QA plan's effectiveness?
<--- Score

101. What can you control?
<--- Score

102. What is your plan to assess your security risks?
<--- Score

Add up total points for this section:
_ _ _ _ _ = Total points for this section

Divided by: _ _ _ _ _ _ (number of statements answered) = _ _ _ _ _ _

Average score for this section

Transfer your score to the sales strategy
Index at the beginning of the Self-
Assessment.

CRITERION #7: SUSTAIN:

INTENT: Retain the benefits.

In my belief, the answer to this question is clearly defined:

5 Strongly Agree

4 Agree

3 Neutral

2 Disagree

1 Strongly Disagree

1. What are the rules and assumptions your industry operates under? What if the opposite were true?
<--- Score

2. Why should people listen to you?
<--- Score

3. What trouble can you get into?
<--- Score

4. How do you foster the skills, knowledge, talents,

attributes, and characteristics you want to have?
<--- Score

5. Who have you, as a company, historically been when you've been at your best?
<--- Score

6. Is sales strategy realistic, or are you setting yourself up for failure?
<--- Score

7. Would you rather sell to knowledgeable and informed customers or to uninformed customers?
<--- Score

8. What unique value proposition (UVP) do you offer?
<--- Score

9. Are you / should you be revolutionary or evolutionary?
<--- Score

10. What sales strategy modifications can you make work for you?
<--- Score

11. How do you determine the key elements that affect sales strategy workforce satisfaction, how are these elements determined for different workforce groups and segments?
<--- Score

12. How do you govern and fulfill your societal responsibilities?
<--- Score

13. How do you know if you are successful?
<--- Score

14. What are the success criteria that will indicate that sales strategy objectives have been met and the benefits delivered?
<--- Score

15. Do you think sales strategy accomplishes the goals you expect it to accomplish?
<--- Score

16. What is the craziest thing you can do?
<--- Score

17. Who is responsible for errors?
<--- Score

18. Why is it important to have senior management support for a sales strategy project?
<--- Score

19. At what moment would you think; Will I get fired?
<--- Score

20. In the past year, what have you done (or could you have done) to increase the accurate perception of your company/brand as ethical and honest?
<--- Score

21. How do you proactively clarify deliverables and sales strategy quality expectations?
<--- Score

22. Sales strategy: does the vendor have an innovative partner strategy, attractive pricing,

flexible and clear product packaging, and a strong land-and-expand and enterprise sales model?
<--- Score

23. How will you ensure you get what you expected?
<--- Score

24. Is sales strategy dependent on the successful delivery of a current project?
<--- Score

25. What should you stop doing?
<--- Score

26. What is a feasible sequencing of reform initiatives over time?
<--- Score

27. Are you changing as fast as the world around you?
<--- Score

28. Instead of going to current contacts for new ideas, what if you reconnected with dormant contacts-- the people you used to know? If you were going reactivate a dormant tie, who would it be?
<--- Score

29. What is the estimated value of the project?
<--- Score

30. If your company went out of business tomorrow, would anyone who doesn't get a paycheck here care?
<--- Score

31. What stupid rule would you most like to kill?
<--- Score

32. Think of your sales strategy project, what are the main functions?
<--- Score

33. What is your question? Why?
<--- Score

34. How can you negotiate sales strategy successfully with a stubborn boss, an irate client, or a deceitful coworker?
<--- Score

35. What must you excel at?
<--- Score

36. What are the usability implications of sales strategy actions?
<--- Score

37. Why is sales strategy important for you now?
<--- Score

38. Who are your customers?
<--- Score

39. Who do we want your customers to become?
<--- Score

40. What is something you believe that nearly no one agrees with you on?
<--- Score

41. How important is sales strategy to the user organizations mission?
<--- Score

42. Why will customers want to buy your organizations products/services?
<--- Score

43. What sales strategy will be employed?
<--- Score

44. Is it economical; do you have the time and money?
<--- Score

45. What is the purpose of sales strategy in relation to the mission?
<--- Score

46. What are internal and external sales strategy relations?
<--- Score

47. If you do not follow, then how to lead?
<--- Score

48. How do you maintain sales strategy's Integrity?
<--- Score

49. How do customers see your organization?
<--- Score

50. Is there any reason to believe the opposite of my current belief?
<--- Score

51. What would have to be true for the option on the table to be the best possible choice?
<--- Score

52. What are the long-term sales strategy goals?
<--- Score

53. How do you lead with sales strategy in mind?
<--- Score

54. Who is on the team?
<--- Score

55. Whom among your colleagues do you trust, and for what?
<--- Score

56. What is it like to work for you?
<--- Score

57. What are you trying to prove to yourself, and how might it be hijacking your life and business success?
<--- Score

58. What projects are going on in the organization today, and what resources are those projects using from the resource pools?
<--- Score

59. What have you done to protect your business from competitive encroachment?
<--- Score

60. What are the business goals sales strategy is aiming to achieve?
<--- Score

61. Who will determine interim and final deadlines?
<--- Score

62. How will you know that the sales strategy project has been successful?

<--- Score

63. How do you keep the momentum going?

<--- Score

64. What may be the consequences for the performance of an organization if all stakeholders are not consulted regarding sales strategy?

<--- Score

65. What is the overall business strategy?

<--- Score

66. Which functions and people interact with the supplier and or customer?

<--- Score

67. How long will it take to change?

<--- Score

68. How do you make it meaningful in connecting sales strategy with what users do day-to-day?

<--- Score

69. How much contingency will be available in the budget?

<--- Score

70. How will you insure seamless interoperability of sales strategy moving forward?

<--- Score

71. What are the potential basics of sales strategy fraud?

<--- Score

72. Do you have the right people on the bus?
<--- Score

73. How do you manage sales strategy Knowledge
Management (KM)?
<--- Score

74. What is the source of the strategies for sales
strategy strengthening and reform?
<--- Score

75. Are you maintaining a past–present–future
perspective throughout the sales strategy discussion?
<--- Score

76. Are you satisfied with your current role? If not,
what is missing from it?
<--- Score

77. What did you miss in the interview for the worst
hire you ever made?
<--- Score

78. What is effective sales strategy?
<--- Score

79. If you weren't already in this business, would you
enter it today? And if not, what are you going to do
about it?
<--- Score

80. How do you cross-sell and up-sell your sales
strategy success?
<--- Score

81. Marketing budgets are tighter, consumers are more skeptical, and social media has changed forever the way we talk about sales strategy, how do you gain traction?
<--- Score

82. What are specific sales strategy rules to follow?
<--- Score

83. Who else should you help?
<--- Score

84. What is your sales strategy strategy?
<--- Score

85. Is there any existing sales strategy governance structure?
<--- Score

86. What happens when a new employee joins the organization?
<--- Score

87. What are strategies for increasing support and reducing opposition?
<--- Score

88. Can you maintain your growth without detracting from the factors that have contributed to your success?
<--- Score

89. What are current sales strategy paradigms?
<--- Score

90. What role does communication play in the success or failure of a sales strategy project?
<--- Score

91. Are you making progress, and are you making progress as sales strategy leaders?
<--- Score

92. What would you recommend your friend do if he/she were facing this dilemma?
<--- Score

93. If you had to leave your organization for a year and the only communication you could have with employees/colleagues was a single paragraph, what would you write?
<--- Score

94. Do you have enough freaky customers in your portfolio pushing you to the limit day in and day out?
<--- Score

95. Is the sales strategy organization completing tasks effectively and efficiently?
<--- Score

96. What are the key enablers to make this sales strategy move?
<--- Score

97. What trophy do you want on your mantle?
<--- Score

98. How do you listen to customers to obtain actionable information?
<--- Score

99. Who will manage the integration of tools?
<--- Score

100. What is the funding source for this project?
<--- Score

101. Are you paying enough attention to the partners your company depends on to succeed?
<--- Score

102. Who are the key stakeholders?
<--- Score

103. Do you have the right capabilities and capacities?
<--- Score

104. Do you say no to customers for no reason?
<--- Score

105. When information truly is ubiquitous, when reach and connectivity are completely global, when computing resources are infinite, and when a whole new set of impossibilities are not only possible, but happening, what will that do to your business?
<--- Score

106. Do you see more potential in people than they do in themselves?
<--- Score

107. Is your basic point _____ or _____?
<--- Score

108. What are the phases of your inbound sales strategy?

<--- Score

109. If no one would ever find out about your accomplishments, how would you lead differently?
<--- Score

110. Who will provide the final approval of sales strategy deliverables?
<--- Score

111. Can you do all this work?
<--- Score

112. Who is responsible for ensuring appropriate resources (time, people and money) are allocated to sales strategy?
<--- Score

113. Who will be responsible for deciding whether sales strategy goes ahead or not after the initial investigations?
<--- Score

114. Are assumptions made in sales strategy stated explicitly?
<--- Score

115. Why should you adopt a sales strategy framework?
<--- Score

116. How do you go about securing sales strategy?
<--- Score

117. Do sales strategy rules make a reasonable demand on a users capabilities?

<--- Score

118. Did your employees make progress today?
<--- Score

119. What are the short and long-term sales strategy goals?
<--- Score

120. Are you using a design thinking approach and integrating Innovation, sales strategy Experience, and Brand Value?
<--- Score

121. How do you track customer value, profitability or financial return, organizational success, and sustainability?
<--- Score

122. Do you have an implicit bias for capital investments over people investments?
<--- Score

123. Are the criteria for selecting recommendations stated?
<--- Score

124. What is your formula for success in sales strategy ?
<--- Score

125. How do senior leaders deploy your organizations vision and values through your leadership system, to the workforce, to key suppliers and partners, and to customers and other stakeholders, as appropriate?
<--- Score

126. How can you become the company that would put you out of business?
<--- Score

127. What have been your experiences in defining long range sales strategy goals?
<--- Score

128. What knowledge, skills and characteristics mark a good sales strategy project manager?
<--- Score

129. Which sales strategy goals are the most important?
<--- Score

130. What relationships among sales strategy trends do you perceive?
<--- Score

131. How do you provide a safe environment -physically and emotionally?
<--- Score

132. Do you have past sales strategy successes?
<--- Score

133. Why do and why don't your customers like your organization?
<--- Score

134. What is the kind of project structure that would be appropriate for your sales strategy project, should it be formal and complex, or can it be less formal and relatively simple?

<--- Score

135. Is your strategy driving your strategy? Or is the way in which you allocate resources driving your strategy?
<--- Score

136. Operational - will it work?
<--- Score

137. Who is responsible for sales strategy?
<--- Score

138. Where can you break convention?
<--- Score

139. What are you challenging?
<--- Score

140. What is the range of capabilities?
<--- Score

141. How do you foster innovation?
<--- Score

142. What is the recommended frequency of auditing?
<--- Score

143. What are your personal philosophies regarding sales strategy and how do they influence your work?
<--- Score

144. How likely is it that a customer would recommend your company to a friend or colleague?
<--- Score

145. In retrospect, of the projects that you pulled the plug on, what percent do you wish had been allowed to keep going, and what percent do you wish had ended earlier?
<--- Score

146. What management system can you use to leverage the sales strategy experience, ideas, and concerns of the people closest to the work to be done?
<--- Score

147. Will there be any necessary staff changes (redundancies or new hires)?
<--- Score

148. What is the overall talent health of your organization as a whole at senior levels, and for each organization reporting to a member of the Senior Leadership Team?
<--- Score

149. Who are four people whose careers you have enhanced?
<--- Score

150. What is an unauthorized commitment?
<--- Score

151. What business benefits will sales strategy goals deliver if achieved?
<--- Score

152. Do you know what you are doing? And who do you call if you don't?
<--- Score

153. Can the schedule be done in the given time?
<--- Score

154. Who do you think the world wants your organization to be?
<--- Score

155. Has implementation been effective in reaching specified objectives so far?
<--- Score

156. If you got fired and a new hire took your place, what would she do different?
<--- Score

157. In a project to restructure sales strategy outcomes, which stakeholders would you involve?
<--- Score

158. What one word do you want to own in the minds of your customers, employees, and partners?
<--- Score

159. How do you transition from the baseline to the target?
<--- Score

160. What threat is sales strategy addressing?
<--- Score

161. What information is critical to your organization that your executives are ignoring?
<--- Score

162. Are the assumptions believable and achievable?

<--- Score

163. Are all key stakeholders present at all Structured Walkthroughs?
<--- Score

164. What are your most important goals for the strategic sales strategy objectives?
<--- Score

165. Are you relevant? Will you be relevant five years from now? Ten?
<--- Score

166. How do you accomplish your long range sales strategy goals?
<--- Score

167. What is your BATNA (best alternative to a negotiated agreement)?
<--- Score

168. What are the top 3 things at the forefront of your sales strategy agendas for the next 3 years?
<--- Score

169. What happens if you do not have enough funding?
<--- Score

170. How can you incorporate support to ensure safe and effective use of sales strategy into the services that you provide?
<--- Score

171. Whose voice (department, ethnic group, women,

older workers, etc) might you have missed hearing from in your company, and how might you amplify this voice to create positive momentum for your business?
<--- Score

172. Who uses your product in ways you never expected?
<--- Score

173. How do you assess the sales strategy pitfalls that are inherent in implementing it?
<--- Score

174. How do you deal with sales strategy changes?
<--- Score

175. Political -is anyone trying to undermine this project?
<--- Score

176. What counts that you are not counting?
<--- Score

177. Do you think you know, or do you know you know ?
<--- Score

178. How is implementation research currently incorporated into each of your goals?
<--- Score

179. What goals did you miss?
<--- Score

180. Is a sales strategy team work effort in place?

<--- Score

181. What will be the consequences to the stakeholder (financial, reputation etc) if sales strategy does not go ahead or fails to deliver the objectives?
<--- Score

182. How do you stay inspired?
<--- Score

183. What sales strategy skills are most important?
<--- Score

184. What you are going to do to affect the numbers?
<--- Score

185. Do you feel that more should be done in the sales strategy area?
<--- Score

186. How do you ensure that implementations of sales strategy products are done in a way that ensures safety?
<--- Score

187. What potential megatrends could make your business model obsolete?
<--- Score

188. How do you set sales strategy stretch targets and how do you get people to not only participate in setting these stretch targets but also that they strive to achieve these?
<--- Score

189. Is your global account sales strategy truly

global?
<--- Score

190. What are the gaps in your knowledge and experience?
<--- Score

191. Who is the main stakeholder, with ultimate responsibility for driving sales strategy forward?
<--- Score

192. How can you become more high-tech but still be high touch?
<--- Score

193. If you were responsible for initiating and implementing major changes in your organization, what steps might you take to ensure acceptance of those changes?
<--- Score

194. Is there a work around that you can use?
<--- Score

195. How do you create buy-in?
<--- Score

196. What new services of functionality will be implemented next with sales strategy ?
<--- Score

197. Will it be accepted by users?
<--- Score

198. If you had to rebuild your organization without any traditional competitive advantages (i.e., no killer

technology, promising research, innovative product/
service delivery model, etcetera), how would your
people have to approach their work and collaborate
together in order to create the necessary conditions
for success?
<--- Score

199. Is maximizing sales strategy protection the same
as minimizing sales strategy loss?
<--- Score

200. What are the challenges?
<--- Score

201. How are you doing compared to your industry?
<--- Score

202. How much does sales strategy help?
<--- Score

Add up total points for this section:
_____ = Total points for this section

Divided by: _____ (number of
statements answered) = _____
Average score for this section

Transfer your score to the sales strategy
Index at the beginning of the Self-
Assessment.

Sales Strategy and Managing Projects, Criteria for Project Managers:

1.0 Initiating Process Group: Sales Strategy

1. Did the Sales Strategy project team have the right skills?

2. Have requirements been tested, approved, and fulfill the Sales Strategy project scope?

3. If action is called for, what form should it take?

4. Based on your Sales Strategy project communication management plan, what worked well?

5. When are the deliverables to be generated in each phase?

6. How can you make your needs known?

7. Were resources available as planned?

8. What were the challenges that you encountered during the execution of a previous Sales Strategy project that you would not want to repeat?

9. Do you understand the quality and control criteria that must be achieved for successful Sales Strategy project completion?

10. Information sharing?

11. How do you help others satisfy needs?

12. What are the tools and techniques to be used in

each phase?

13. Specific - is the objective clear in terms of what, how, when, and where the situation will be changed?

14. What are the short and long term implications?

15. Are there resources to maintain and support the outcome of the Sales Strategy project?

16. Establishment of pm office?

17. Which six sigma dmaic phase focuses on why and how defects and errors occur?

18. Do you know the Sales Strategy projects goal, purpose and objectives?

19. Realistic - are the desired results expressed in a way that the team will be motivated and believe that the required level of involvement will be obtained?

20. The Sales Strategy project managers have maximum authority in which type of organization?

1.1 Project Charter: Sales Strategy

21. How do you manage integration?

22. Why is a Sales Strategy project Charter used?

23. What changes can you make to improve?

24. Environmental stewardship and sustainability considerations: what is the process that will be used to ensure compliance with the environmental stewardship policy?

25. What goes into your Sales Strategy project Charter?

26. Why is it important?

27. Why the improvements?

28. How will you know that a change is an improvement?

29. Assumptions: what factors, for planning purposes, are you considering to be true?

30. For whom?

31. Dependent Sales Strategy projects: what Sales Strategy projects must be underway or completed before this Sales Strategy project can be successful?

32. What is the most common tool for helping define the detail?

33. Did your Sales Strategy project ask for this?

34. What are the assigned resources?

35. Run it as as a startup?

36. Why have you chosen the aim you have set forth?

37. Why use a Sales Strategy project charter?

38. Why Outsource?

39. Must Have?

1.2 Stakeholder Register: Sales Strategy

40. What & Why?

41. How should employers make voices heard?

42. How will reports be created?

43. How much influence do they have on the Sales Strategy project?

44. How big is the gap?

45. What is the power of the stakeholder?

46. Who is managing stakeholder engagement?

47. What are the major Sales Strategy project milestones requiring communications or providing communications opportunities?

48. What opportunities exist to provide communications?

49. Is your organization ready for change?

50. Who wants to talk about Security?

51. Who are the stakeholders?

1.3 Stakeholder Analysis Matrix: Sales Strategy

52. Is there evidence that demonstrates the impact of education on the Sales Strategy projects outcomes?

53. Who can contribute financial or technical resources towards the work?

54. Are you going to weigh the stakeholders?

55. Who is most dependent on the resources at stake?

56. Market demand?

57. Processes, systems, it, communications?

58. What actions can be taken to reduce or mitigate risk?

59. Who has control over whom?

60. How do rules, behaviors affect stakes?

61. Which conditions out of the control of the management are crucial for the achievement of the immediate objective?

62. Identify the stakeholders levels most frequently used –or at least sought– in your Sales Strategy projects and for which purpose?

63. How to measure the achievement of the

Immediate Objective?

64. How much do resources cost?

65. Seasonality, weather effects?

66. It developments?

67. Who has been involved in the area (thematic or geographic) in the past?

68. Guiding question: what is the issue at stake?

69. What is social & public accountability ?

70. Which resources are required?

71. What obstacles does your organization face?

2.0 Planning Process Group: Sales Strategy

72. The Sales Strategy project charter is created in which Sales Strategy project management process group?

73. Is the schedule for the set products being met?

74. To what extent and in what ways are the Sales Strategy project contributing to progress towards organizational reform?

75. You are creating your WBS and find that you keep decomposing tasks into smaller and smaller units. How can you tell when you are done?

76. How are the principles of aid effectiveness (ownership, alignment, management for development results and mutual responsibility) being applied in the Sales Strategy project?

77. What factors are contributing to progress or delay in the achievement of products and results?

78. Is the Sales Strategy project making progress in helping to achieve the set results?

79. When developing the estimates for Sales Strategy project phases, you choose to add the individual estimates for the activities that comprise each phase. What type of estimation method are you using?

80. Did the program design/ implementation strategy adequately address the planning stage necessary to set up structures, hire staff etc.?

81. To what extent are the participating departments coordinating with each other?

82. How should needs be met?

83. In what ways can the governance of the Sales Strategy project be improved so that it has greater likelihood of achieving future sustainability?

84. How will you know you did it?

85. How are it Sales Strategy projects different?

86. Is your organization showing technical capacity and leadership commitment to keep working with the Sales Strategy project and to repeat it?

87. Are the follow-up indicators relevant and do they meet the quality needed to measure the outputs and outcomes of the Sales Strategy project?

88. In what way has the Sales Strategy project come up with innovative measures for problem-solving?

89. Sales Strategy project assessment; why did you do this Sales Strategy project?

90. What do they need to know about the Sales Strategy project?

91. To what extent has the intervention strategy been adapted to the areas of intervention in which it is

being implemented?

2.1 Project Management Plan: Sales Strategy

92. Are the proposed Sales Strategy project purposes different than a previously authorized Sales Strategy project?

93. Are there any client staffing expectations?

94. What are the deliverables?

95. Are calculations and results of analyzes essentially correct?

96. Where does all this information come from?

97. What data/reports/tools/etc. do your PMs need?

98. Do there need to be organizational changes?

99. What would you do differently?

100. Are there non-structural buyout or relocation recommendations?

101. Are there any scope changes proposed for a previously authorized Sales Strategy project?

102. Has the selected plan been formulated using cost effectiveness and incremental analysis techniques?

103. What is Sales Strategy project scope management?

104. Is the budget realistic?

105. When is a Sales Strategy project management plan created?

106. Do the proposed changes from the Sales Strategy project include any significant risks to safety?

107. Does the implementation plan have an appropriate division of responsibilities?

108. What happened during the process that you found interesting?

109. Are the existing and future without-plan conditions reasonable and appropriate?

110. What should you drop in order to add something new?

2.2 Scope Management Plan: Sales Strategy

111. How much money have you spent?

112. Has a Sales Strategy project Communications Plan been developed?

113. Is each item clearly and completely defined?

114. Are the schedule estimates reasonable given the Sales Strategy project?

115. Time estimation – how much time will be needed?

116. Without-plan conditions?

117. How do you handle uncertainty or conflict?

118. What is the relative power of the Sales Strategy project manager?

119. What does the critical path really mean?

120. Is stakeholder involvement adequate?

121. Are non-critical path items updated and agreed upon with the teams?

122. Have key stakeholders been identified?

123. Are stakeholders aware and supportive of

the principles and practices of modern software estimation?

124. Are corrective actions taken when actual results are substantially different from detailed Sales Strategy project plan (variances)?

125. Have Sales Strategy project management standards and procedures been identified / established and documented?

126. Will the Sales Strategy project deliverables become accepted in writing?

127. What are the risks that could significantly affect the scope of the Sales Strategy project?

128. Can the Sales Strategy project team do several activities in parallel?

129. What went wrong?

130. What work performance data will be captured?

2.3 Requirements Management Plan: Sales Strategy

131. What information regarding the Sales Strategy project requirements will be reported?

132. Who is responsible for quantifying the Sales Strategy project requirements?

133. Do you really need to write this document at all?

134. Will the product release be stable and mature enough to be deployed in the user community?

135. Subject to change control?

136. Are actual resources expenditures versus planned expenditures acceptable?

137. Do you have price sheets and a methodology for determining the total proposal cost?

138. Who will do the reporting and to whom will reports be delivered?

139. Does the Sales Strategy project have a Change Control process?

140. Did you avoid subjective, flowery or non-specific statements?

141. Who will initially review the Sales Strategy project work or products to ensure it meets the applicable

acceptance criteria?

142. Business analysis scope?

143. Who has the authority to reject Sales Strategy project requirements?

144. Will you document changes to requirements?

145. Is infrastructure setup part of your Sales Strategy project?

146. When and how will a requirements baseline be established in this Sales Strategy project?

147. How will the information be distributed?

148. Did you get proper approvals?

149. What are you counting on?

150. How will requirements be managed?

2.4 Requirements Documentation: Sales Strategy

151. Where are business rules being captured?

152. How will the proposed Sales Strategy project help?

153. How will they be documented / shared?

154. What are the attributes of a customer?

155. Can you check system requirements?

156. Completeness. are all functions required by the customer included?

157. How much does requirements engineering cost?

158. How linear / iterative is your Requirements Gathering process (or will it be)?

159. What images does it conjure?

160. Basic work/business process; high-level, what is being touched?

161. How can you document system requirements?

162. Is the requirement realistically testable?

163. What is effective documentation?

164. Consistency. are there any requirements conflicts?

165. What is your Elevator Speech?

166. What happens when requirements are wrong?

167. Have the benefits identified with the system being identified clearly?

168. Where do you define what is a customer, what are the attributes of customer?

169. Are all functions required by the customer included?

170. Has requirements gathering uncovered information that would necessitate changes?

2.5 Requirements Traceability Matrix: Sales Strategy

171. How small is small enough?

172. Is there a requirements traceability process in place?

173. How do you manage scope?

174. What percentage of Sales Strategy projects are producing traceability matrices between requirements and other work products?

175. What are the chronologies, contingencies, consequences, criteria?

176. Describe the process for approving requirements so they can be added to the traceability matrix and Sales Strategy project work can be performed. Will the Sales Strategy project requirements become approved in writing?

177. How will it affect the stakeholders personally in career?

178. Will you use a Requirements Traceability Matrix?

179. Why do you manage scope?

180. Do you have a clear understanding of all subcontracts in place?

181. What is the WBS?

182. Why use a WBS?

2.6 Project Scope Statement: Sales Strategy

183. Will the qa related information be reported regularly as part of the status reporting mechanisms?

184. Are the meetings set up to have assigned note takers that will add action/issues to the issue list?

185. Which risks does the Sales Strategy project focus on?

186. What are the defined meeting materials?

187. Has everyone approved the Sales Strategy projects scope statement?

188. Is there an information system for the Sales Strategy project?

189. How will you verify the accuracy of the work of the Sales Strategy project, and what constitutes acceptance of the deliverables?

190. Identify how your team and you will create the Sales Strategy project scope statement and the work breakdown structure (WBS). Document how you will create the Sales Strategy project scope statement and WBS, and make sure you answer the following questions: In defining Sales Strategy project scope and the WBS, will you and your Sales Strategy project team be using methods defined by your organization, methods defined by the Sales Strategy project

management office (PMO), or other methods?

191. Does the scope statement still need some clarity?

192. Has a method and process for requirement tracking been developed?

193. Elements of scope management that deal with concept development ?

194. Who will you recommend approve the change, and when do you recommend the change reviews occur?

195. Is the Sales Strategy project sponsor function identified and defined?

196. Is the plan for your organization of the Sales Strategy project resources adequate?

197. What is the product of this Sales Strategy project?

198. Are there completion/verification criteria defined for each task producing an output?

199. What are the major deliverables of the Sales Strategy project?

200. Is an issue management process documented and filed?

2.7 Assumption and Constraint Log: Sales Strategy

201. Are formal code reviews conducted?

202. Are there cosmetic errors that hinder readability and comprehension?

203. Have adequate resources been provided by management to ensure Sales Strategy project success?

204. What other teams / processes would be impacted by changes to the current process, and how?

205. Does the system design reflect the requirements?

206. Are there nonconformance issues?

207. Are there processes in place to ensure internal consistency between the source code components?

208. Do documented requirements exist for all critical components and areas, including technical, business, interfaces, performance, security and conversion requirements?

209. Would known impacts serve as impediments?

210. How can constraints be violated?

211. Does the document/deliverable meet general requirements (for example, statement of work) for all

deliverables?

212. Is there a Steering Committee in place?

213. Is the process working, and people are not executing in compliance of the process?

214. What strengths do you have?

215. Is the amount of effort justified by the anticipated value of forming a new process?

216. What worked well?

217. Is staff trained on the software technologies that are being used on the Sales Strategy project?

218. When can log be discarded?

219. Are requirements management tracking tools and procedures in place?

220. Contradictory information between different documents?

2.8 Work Breakdown Structure: Sales Strategy

221. How far down?

222. What has to be done?

223. Is it still viable?

224. Who has to do it?

225. When does it have to be done?

226. When do you stop?

227. Do you need another level?

228. How many levels?

229. Can you make it?

230. How much detail?

231. Is it a change in scope?

232. Where does it take place?

233. Is the work breakdown structure (wbs) defined and is the scope of the Sales Strategy project clear with assigned deliverable owners?

234. How big is a work-package?

235. When would you develop a Work Breakdown Structure?

236. How will you and your Sales Strategy project team define the Sales Strategy projects scope and work breakdown structure?

237. Why would you develop a Work Breakdown Structure?

2.9 WBS Dictionary: Sales Strategy

238. Appropriate work authorization documents which subdivide the contractual effort and responsibilities, within functional organizations?

239. Are procedures in existence that control replanning of unopened work packages, and are corresponding procedures adhered to?

240. Are overhead cost budgets established for each organization which has authority to incur overhead costs?

241. Are work packages reasonably short in time duration or do they have adequate objective indicators/milestones to minimize subjectivity of the in process work evaluation?

242. Are records maintained to show how management reserves are used?

243. Is subcontracted work defined and identified to the appropriate subcontractor within the proper WBS element?

244. Does the scheduling system identify in a timely manner the status of work?

245. Is all budget available as management reserve identified and excluded from the performance measurement baseline?

246. Actual cost of work performed?

247. Incurrence of actual indirect costs in excess of budgets, by element of expense?

248. Contemplated overhead expenditure for each period based on the best information currently available?

249. Do the lines of authority for incurring indirect costs correspond to the lines of responsibility for management control of the same components of costs?

250. Are budgets or values assigned to work packages and planning packages in terms of dollars, hours, or other measurable units?

251. Software specification, development, integration, and testing, licenses ?

252. Does the contractors system include procedures for measuring the performance of critical subcontractors?

253. Are meaningful indicators identified for use in measuring the status of cost and schedule performance?

254. Detailed schedules which support control account and work package start and completion dates/events?

255. Do work packages consist of discrete tasks which are adequately described?

256. Are detailed work packages planned as far in

advance as practicable?

2.10 Schedule Management Plan: Sales Strategy

257. Has the scope management document been updated and distributed to help prevent scope creep?

258. Are the appropriate IT resources adequate to meet planned commitments?

259. Are post milestone Sales Strategy project reviews (PMPR) conducted with your organization at least once a year?

260. Are internal Sales Strategy project status meetings held at reasonable intervals?

261. Are multiple estimation methods being employed?

262. Why conduct schedule analysis?

263. Alignment to strategic goals & objectives?

264. What will be the format of the schedule model?

265. Does the Sales Strategy project have a Quality Culture?

266. Have reserves been created to address risks?

267. Were Sales Strategy project team members involved in the development of activity & task decomposition?

268. Are the constraints or deadlines associated with the task accurate?

269. Which status reports are received per the Sales Strategy project Plan?

270. Has the budget been baselined?

271. Sales Strategy project definition & scope?

272. What tools and techniques will be used to estimate activity resources?

273. Does all Sales Strategy project documentation reside in a common repository for easy access?

274. List all schedule constraints here. Must the Sales Strategy project be complete by a specified date?

275. Have the key functions and capabilities been defined and assigned to each release or iteration?

276. Does the detailed work plan match the complexity of tasks with the capabilities of personnel?

2.11 Activity List: Sales Strategy

277. What are the critical bottleneck activities?

278. How do you determine the late start (LS) for each activity?

279. Where will it be performed?

280. Who will perform the work?

281. What will be performed?

282. In what sequence?

283. For other activities, how much delay can be tolerated?

284. When do the individual activities need to start and finish?

285. Is there anything planned that does not need to be here?

286. What did not go as well?

287. How will it be performed?

288. How difficult will it be to do specific activities on this Sales Strategy project?

289. What went right?

290. The wbs is developed as part of a joint planning

session. and how do you know that youhave done this right?

291. What went well?

292. What is the total time required to complete the Sales Strategy project if no delays occur?

293. What is the probability the Sales Strategy project can be completed in xx weeks?

294. When will the work be performed?

2.12 Activity Attributes: Sales Strategy

295. How many days do you need to complete the work scope with a limit of X number of resources?

296. Resources to accomplish the work?

297. Are the required resources available?

298. How do you manage time?

299. Have you identified the Activity Leveling Priority code value on each activity?

300. Are the required resources available or need to be acquired?

301. Can more resources be added?

302. How else could the items be grouped?

303. Has management defined a definite timeframe for the turnaround or Sales Strategy project window?

304. What activity do you think you should spend the most time on?

305. Time for overtime?

306. What is the general pattern here?

307. What is your organizations history in doing

similar activities?

308. How much activity detail is required?

309. How difficult will it be to complete specific activities on this Sales Strategy project?

310. What conclusions/generalizations can you draw from this?

311. Would you consider either of corresponding activities an outlier?

2.13 Milestone List: Sales Strategy

312. What specific improvements did you make to the Sales Strategy project proposal since the previous time?

313. Can you derive how soon can the whole Sales Strategy project finish?

314. Calculate how long can activity be delayed?

315. How late can each activity be finished and started?

316. Loss of key staff?

317. Insurmountable weaknesses?

318. How will you get the word out to customers?

319. Effects on core activities, distraction?

320. Describe the industry you are in and the market growth opportunities. What is the market for your technology, product or service?

321. New USPs?

322. What would happen if a delivery of material was one week late?

323. Vital contracts and partners?

324. Which path is the critical path?

325. What has been done so far?

326. Usps (unique selling points)?

327. Who will manage the Sales Strategy project on a day-to-day basis?

328. Describe your organizations strengths and core competencies. What factors will make your organization succeed?

329. Environmental effects?

2.14 Network Diagram: Sales Strategy

330. Exercise: what is the probability that the Sales Strategy project duration will exceed xx weeks?

331. Are the gantt chart and/or network diagram updated periodically and used to assess the overall Sales Strategy project timetable?

332. Can you calculate the confidence level?

333. How difficult will it be to do specific activities on this Sales Strategy project?

334. If x is long, what would be the completion time if you break x into two parallel parts of y weeks and z weeks?

335. What is the lowest cost to complete this Sales Strategy project in xx weeks?

336. If a current contract exists, can you provide the vendor name, contract start, and contract expiration date?

337. What are the tools?

338. Planning: who, how long, what to do?

339. What activities must occur simultaneously with this activity?

340. What controls the start and finish of a job?

341. Will crashing x weeks return more in benefits than it costs?

342. Where do schedules come from?

343. Why must you schedule milestones, such as reviews, throughout the Sales Strategy project?

344. How confident can you be in your milestone dates and the delivery date?

345. What is the completion time?

346. What job or jobs could run concurrently?

347. What are the Key Success Factors?

348. What to do and When?

2.15 Activity Resource Requirements: Sales Strategy

349. Organizational Applicability?

350. Other support in specific areas?

351. What are constraints that you might find during the Human Resource Planning process?

352. When does monitoring begin?

353. Why do you do that?

354. How many signatures do you require on a check and does this match what is in your policy and procedures?

355. Do you use tools like decomposition and rolling-wave planning to produce the activity list and other outputs?

356. Are there unresolved issues that need to be addressed?

357. How do you handle petty cash?

358. Anything else?

359. What is the Work Plan Standard?

360. Which logical relationship does the PDM use most often?

2.16 Resource Breakdown Structure: Sales Strategy

361. When do they need the information?

362. The list could probably go on, but, the thing that you would most like to know is, How long & How much?

363. What is the number one predictor of a groups productivity?

364. Why is this important?

365. Who needs what information?

366. What defines a successful Sales Strategy project?

367. What are the requirements for resource data?

368. Goals for the Sales Strategy project. What is each stakeholders desired outcome for the Sales Strategy project?

369. What is each stakeholders desired outcome for the Sales Strategy project?

370. Who will use the system?

371. Changes based on input from stakeholders?

372. Why do you do it?

373. How should the information be delivered?

374. How can this help you with team building?

375. What defines a successful Sales Strategy project?

376. What is the difference between % Complete and % work?

377. Which resources should be in the resource pool?

378. Who delivers the information?

2.17 Activity Duration Estimates: Sales Strategy

379. What functions does this software provide that cannot be done easily using other tools such as a spreadsheet or database?

380. Research risk management software. Are many products available?

381. Total slack can be calculated by which equations?

382. How is the Sales Strategy project doing?

383. Are procurement documents used to solicit accurate and complete proposals from prospective sellers?

384. Why should Sales Strategy project managers strive to make jobs look easy?

385. What distinguishes one organization from another in this area?

386. Are changes to the scope managed according to defined procedures?

387. Does the case present a realistic scenario?

388. How does Sales Strategy project integration management relate to the Sales Strategy project life cycle, stakeholders, and the other Sales Strategy project management knowledge areas?

389. Is a contract change control system defined to manage changes to contract terms and conditions?

390. Have most organizations benefited from outsourcing?

391. How does Sales Strategy project management relate to other disciplines?

392. How difficult will it be to do specific activities on this Sales Strategy project?

393. What are the ways to create and distribute Sales Strategy project performance information?

394. Which does one need in order to complete schedule development?

395. Sales Strategy project manager is using weighted average duration estimates to perform schedule network analysis. Which type of mathematical analysis is being used?

396. Is a provider selected based upon defined evaluation criteria?

2.18 Duration Estimating Worksheet: Sales Strategy

397. What is next?

398. Is a construction detail attached (to aid in explanation)?

399. What work will be included in the Sales Strategy project?

400. Does the Sales Strategy project provide innovative ways for stakeholders to overcome obstacles or deliver better outcomes?

401. Do any colleagues have experience with your organization and/or RFPs?

402. Can the Sales Strategy project be constructed as planned?

403. Value pocket identification & quantification what are value pockets?

404. Is this operation cost effective?

405. What is cost and Sales Strategy project cost management?

406. Small or large Sales Strategy project?

407. What questions do you have?

408. Why estimate time and cost?

409. Why estimate costs?

410. What utility impacts are there?

411. What is an Average Sales Strategy project?

412. Is the Sales Strategy project responsive to community need?

413. What info is needed?

2.19 Project Schedule: Sales Strategy

414. How can slack be negative?

415. How much slack is available in the Sales Strategy project?

416. To what degree is do you feel the entire team was committed to the Sales Strategy project schedule?

417. Meet requirements?

418. How do you know that youhave done this right?

419. Understand the constraints used in preparing the schedule. Are activities connected because logic dictates the order in which others occur?

420. What is risk management?

421. Why is this particularly bad?

422. Did the final product meet or exceed user expectations?

423. Verify that the update is accurate. Are all remaining durations correct?

424. Master Sales Strategy project schedule?

425. Activity charts and bar charts are graphical representations of a Sales Strategy project schedule ...how do they differ?

426. Eliminate unnecessary activities. Are there activities that came from a template or previous Sales Strategy project that are not applicable on this phase of this Sales Strategy project?

427. Schedule/cost recovery?

428. How can you minimize or control changes to Sales Strategy project schedules?

429. Is the structure for tracking the Sales Strategy project schedule well defined and assigned to a specific individual?

430. How do you manage Sales Strategy project Risk?

431. Did the Sales Strategy project come in under budget?

432. What is risk?

2.20 Cost Management Plan: Sales Strategy

433. Is the steering committee active in Sales Strategy project oversight?

434. Designated small business reserve?

435. Time management – how will the schedule impact of changes be estimated and approved?

436. Is it possible to track all classes of Sales Strategy project work (e.g. scheduled, un-scheduled, defect repair, etc.)?

437. Are issues raised, assessed, actioned, and resolved in a timely and efficient manner?

438. Change types and category – What are the types of changes and what are the techniques to report and control changes?

439. Are the Sales Strategy project team members located locally to the users/stakeholders?

440. Are estimating assumptions and constraints captured?

441. Cost management – how will the cost of changes be estimated and controlled?

442. Are Sales Strategy project leaders committed to this Sales Strategy project full time?

443. Have all team members been part of identifying risks?

444. Scope of work – What is the likelihood and extent of potential future changes to the Sales Strategy project scope?

445. Has the Sales Strategy project scope been baselined?

446. Weve met your goals?

447. Personnel with expertise?

448. Has a quality assurance plan been developed for the Sales Strategy project?

449. Is quality monitored from the perspective of the customers needs and expectations?

450. Is there a formal process for updating the Sales Strategy project baseline?

2.21 Activity Cost Estimates: Sales Strategy

451. What makes a good expected result statement?

452. What areas were overlooked on this Sales Strategy project?

453. What is the activity inventory?

454. How do you allocate indirect costs to activities?

455. What cost data should be used to estimate costs during the 2-year follow-up period?

456. Where can you get activity reports?

457. What happens if you cannot produce the documentation for the single audit?

458. How and when do you enter into Sales Strategy project Procurement Management?

459. Are cost subtotals needed?

460. Does the estimator have experience?

461. What is your organizations history in doing similar tasks?

462. Did the Sales Strategy project team have the right skills?

463. What skill level is required to do the job?

464. What makes a good activity description?

465. How many activities should you have?

466. When do you enter into PPM?

467. Why do you manage cost?

468. Is costing method consistent with study goals?

2.22 Cost Estimating Worksheet: Sales Strategy

469. What will others want?

470. What can be included?

471. Will the Sales Strategy project collaborate with the local community and leverage resources?

472. Identify the timeframe necessary to monitor progress and collect data to determine how the selected measure has changed?

473. Ask: are others positioned to know, are others credible, and will others cooperate?

474. What costs are to be estimated?

475. What is the estimated labor cost today based upon this information?

476. Is it feasible to establish a control group arrangement?

477. Is the Sales Strategy project responsive to community need?

478. Does the Sales Strategy project provide innovative ways for stakeholders to overcome obstacles or deliver better outcomes?

479. Can a trend be established from historical

performance data on the selected measure and are the criteria for using trend analysis or forecasting methods met?

480. What additional Sales Strategy project(s) could be initiated as a result of this Sales Strategy project?

481. What happens to any remaining funds not used?

482. Who is best positioned to know and assist in identifying corresponding factors?

483. What is the purpose of estimating?

484. How will the results be shared and to whom?

2.23 Cost Baseline: Sales Strategy

485. Has the Sales Strategy projected annual cost to operate and maintain the product(s) or service(s) been approved and funded?

486. Are there contingencies or conditions related to the acceptance?

487. What can go wrong?

488. How fast?

489. How concrete were original objectives?

490. Does the suggested change request seem to represent a necessary enhancement to the product?

491. Are you asking management for something as a result of this update?

492. Escalation criteria met?

493. Should a more thorough impact analysis be conducted?

494. What is cost and Sales Strategy project cost management?

495. Is there anything unique in this Sales Strategy projects scope statement that will affect resources?

496. What weaknesses do you have?

497. Has training and knowledge transfer of the operations organization been completed?

498. How likely is it to go wrong?

499. Has the appropriate access to relevant data and analysis capability been granted?

500. Is request in line with priorities?

501. What is the consequence?

502. Are procedures defined by which the cost baseline may be changed?

2.24 Quality Management Plan: Sales Strategy

503. Who is responsible?

504. What does it do for you (or to me)?

505. How does training support what is important to your organization and the individual?

506. Were the right locations/samples tested for the right parameters?

507. How are corresponding standards measured?

508. How is staff trained on the recording of field notes?

509. Who do you send data to?

510. With the five whys method, the team considers why the issue being explored occurred. do others then take that initial answer and ask why?

511. How does your organization measure customer satisfaction/dissatisfaction?

512. Documented results available?

513. Who is approving the QAPP?

514. How does your organization decide what to measure?

515. Does the program conduct field testing?

516. How is equipment calibrated?

517. How are senior leaders, employees, and your organization involved in supporting the community?

518. How is staff trained in procedures?

519. Can it be done better?

520. Who gets results of work?

521. If it is out of compliance, should the process be amended or should the Plan be amended?

2.25 Quality Metrics: Sales Strategy

522. What are your organizations next steps?

523. Has it met internal or external standards?

524. Subjective quality component: customer satisfaction, how do you measure it?

525. Is material complete (and does it meet the standards)?

526. Is there a set of procedures to capture, analyze and act on quality metrics?

527. What is the CMS Benchmark?

528. Can you correlate your quality metrics to profitability?

529. What group is empowered to define quality requirements?

530. Is the reporting frequency appropriate?

531. Is quality culture a competitive advantage?

532. When will the Final Guidance will be issued?

533. What are you trying to accomplish?

534. How does one achieve stability?

535. How do you know if everyone is trying to

improve the right things?

536. Were number of defects identified?

537. Which are the right metrics to use?

538. There are many reasons to shore up quality-related metrics, and what metrics are important?

539. Is a risk containment plan in place?

540. Were quality attributes reported?

541. What can manufacturing professionals do to ensure quality is seen as an integral part of the entire product lifecycle?

2.26 Process Improvement Plan: Sales Strategy

542. Are you making progress on the improvement framework?

543. What personnel are the champions for the initiative?

544. Has the time line required to move measurement results from the points of collection to databases or users been established?

545. Does your process ensure quality?

546. Are you following the quality standards?

547. Everyone agrees on what process improvement is, right?

548. To elicit goal statements, do you ask a question such as, What do you want to achieve?

549. Has a process guide to collect the data been developed?

550. What lessons have you learned so far?

551. Where do you want to be?

552. Are there forms and procedures to collect and record the data?

553. Modeling current processes is great, and will you ever see a return on that investment?

554. Purpose of goal: the motive is determined by asking, why do you want to achieve this goal?

555. How do you manage quality?

556. What actions are needed to address the problems and achieve the goals?

557. Have storage and access mechanisms and procedures been determined?

558. Are you making progress on the goals?

559. What personnel are the sponsors for that initiative?

560. Have the frequency of collection and the points in the process where measurements will be made been determined?

561. Where are you now?

2.27 Responsibility Assignment Matrix: Sales Strategy

562. What do you need to implement earned value management?

563. How do you manage remotely to staff in other Divisions?

564. What can you do to improve productivity?

565. What are some important Sales Strategy project communications management tools?

566. The already stated responsible for overhead performance control of related costs?

567. The staff interests – is the group or the person interested in working for this Sales Strategy project?

568. Who is the Sales Strategy project Manager?

569. What is the primary purpose of the human resource plan?

570. What simple tool can you use to help identify and prioritize Sales Strategy project risks that is very low tech and high touch?

571. Does the contractor use objective results, design reviews, and tests to trace schedule?

572. Is it safe to say you can handle more work or

that some tasks you are supposed to do arent worth doing?

573. Changes in the current direct and Sales Strategy projected base?

574. Does the contractors system identify work accomplishment against the schedule plan?

575. What travel needed?

576. Time-phased control account budgets?

577. Which Sales Strategy project management knowledge area is least mature?

578. Budgets assigned to major functional organizations?

579. Most people let you know when others re too busy, and are others really too busy?

2.28 Roles and Responsibilities: Sales Strategy

580. Who is involved?

581. What expectations were met?

582. What specific behaviors did you observe?

583. What areas of supervision are challenging for you?

584. Are Sales Strategy project team roles and responsibilities identified and documented?

585. Who is responsible for implementation activities and where will the functions, roles and responsibilities be defined?

586. Are governance roles and responsibilities documented?

587. What should you do now to ensure that you are meeting all expectations of your current position?

588. What should you do now to ensure that you are exceeding expectations and excelling in your current position?

589. Attainable / achievable: the goal is attainable; can you actually accomplish the goal?

590. Are your policies supportive of a culture of

quality data?

591. What should you highlight for improvement?

592. Is feedback clearly communicated and non-judgmental?

593. Who is responsible for each task?

594. Does your vision/mission support a culture of quality data?

595. Are Sales Strategy project team roles and responsibilities identified and documented?

596. What are your major roles and responsibilities in the area of performance measurement and assessment?

597. Is the data complete?

2.29 Human Resource Management Plan: Sales Strategy

598. Was your organizations estimating methodology being used and followed?

599. Are changes in scope (deliverable commitments) agreed to by all affected groups & individuals?

600. Are corrective actions and variances reported?

601. Quality of people required to meet the forecast needs of the department?

602. How will the Sales Strategy project manage expectations & meet needs and requirements?

603. Do Sales Strategy project managers participating in the Sales Strategy project know the Sales Strategy projects true status first hand?

604. Is this Sales Strategy project carried out in partnership with other groups/organizations?

605. Were escalated issues resolved promptly?

606. Are status reports received per the Sales Strategy project Plan?

607. Are risk triggers captured?

608. Are tasks tracked by hours?

609. Account for the purpose of this Sales Strategy project by describing, at a high-level, what will be done. What is this Sales Strategy project aiming to achieve?

610. Were sponsors and decision makers available when needed outside regularly scheduled meetings?

611. Are the payment terms being followed?

612. Are all resource assumptions documented?

613. Are actuals compared against estimates to analyze and correct variances?

614. Has the Sales Strategy project manager been identified?

615. Does the Sales Strategy project have a Quality Culture?

616. List roles. what commitments have been made?

2.30 Communications Management Plan: Sales Strategy

617. Are stakeholders internal or external?

618. What steps can you take for a positive relationship?

619. What approaches do you use?

620. Which stakeholders are thought leaders, influences, or early adopters?

621. Do you feel more overwhelmed by stakeholders?

622. Do you prepare stakeholder engagement plans?

623. Who is involved as you identify stakeholders?

624. Are there potential barriers between the team and the stakeholder?

625. Why do you manage communications?

626. Conflict resolution -which method when?

627. What is Sales Strategy project communications management?

628. Are there too many who have an interest in some aspect of your work?

629. What approaches to you feel are the best ones to

use?

630. Will messages be directly related to the release strategy or phases of the Sales Strategy project?

631. What communications method?

632. How will the person responsible for executing the communication item be notified?

633. Which stakeholders can influence others?

634. What are the interrelationships?

635. Who have you worked with in past, similar initiatives?

2.31 Risk Management Plan: Sales Strategy

636. Are certain activities taking a long time to complete?

637. Can you stabilize dynamic risk factors?

638. Litigation – what is the probability that lawsuits will cause problems or delays in the Sales Strategy project?

639. Which risks should get the attention?

640. How well were you able to manage your risk before?

641. Are there new risks that mitigation strategies might introduce?

642. What are the chances the event will occur?

643. What is the probability the risk avoidance strategy will be successful?

644. What is the impact to the Sales Strategy project if the item is not resolved in a timely fashion?

645. Who has experience with this?

646. Does the customer understand the software process?

647. Have staff received necessary training?

648. Are some people working on multiple Sales Strategy projects?

649. How is risk identification performed?

650. Financial risk: can your organization afford to undertake the Sales Strategy project?

651. Which is an input to the risk management process?

652. Risk may be made during which step of risk management?

653. How is risk response planning performed?

654. Why do you need to manage Sales Strategy project Risk?

2.32 Risk Register: Sales Strategy

655. Are there any gaps in the evidence?

656. How often will the Risk Management Plan and Risk Register be formally reviewed, and by whom?

657. What may happen or not go according to plan?

658. Are corrective measures implemented as planned?

659. Schedule impact/severity estimated range (workdays) assume the event happens, what is the potential impact?

660. Is further information required before making a decision?

661. Do you require further engagement?

662. Are your objectives at risk?

663. What is the reason for current performance gaps and do the risks and opportunities identified previously account for this?

664. Are there other alternative controls that could be implemented?

665. What should the audit role be in establishing a risk management process?

666. What are your key risks/show istoppers and what

is being done to manage them?

667. Risk documentation: what reporting formats and processes will be used for risk management activities?

668. What is a Risk?

669. What could prevent you delivering on the strategic program objectives and what is being done to mitigate corresponding issues?

670. User involvement: do you have the right users?

671. What are the assumptions and current status that support the assessment of the risk?

672. Manageability – have mitigations to the risk been identified?

673. What is the probability and impact of the risk occurring?

2.33 Probability and Impact Assessment: Sales Strategy

674. How is the risk management process used in practice?

675. Is the Sales Strategy project cutting across the entire organization?

676. Do requirements put excessive performance constraints on the product?

677. Who should be notified of the occurrence of each of the risk indicators?

678. What is the impact if the risk does occur?

679. Is the present organizational structure for handling the Sales Strategy project sufficient?

680. What are the levels of understanding of the future users of the outcome/results of this Sales Strategy project?

681. Why has this particular mode of contracting been chosen?

682. Risks should be identified during which phase of Sales Strategy project management life cycle?

683. How is the Sales Strategy project going to be managed?

684. How will economic events and trends likely affect the Sales Strategy project?

685. Can the Sales Strategy project proceed without assuming the risk?

686. What will be the likely political environment during the life of the Sales Strategy project?

687. Are requirements fully understood by the software engineering team and customers?

688. What will be the likely political situation during the life of the Sales Strategy project?

689. Will there be an increase in the political conservatism?

690. Is a software Sales Strategy project management tool available?

691. Risk urgency assessment -which of your risks could occur soon, or require a longer planning time?

692. What are the preparations required for facing difficulties?

693. How risk averse are you?

2.34 Probability and Impact Matrix: Sales Strategy

694. Do you train all developers in the process?

695. What are ways to measure and evaluate risks?

696. Is the customer willing to establish rapid communication links with the developer?

697. Are the risk data timely and relevant?

698. What are the current demands of the customer?

699. How will economic events and trends likely affect the Sales Strategy project?

700. How will the consumption pattern change?

701. Are Sales Strategy project requirements stable?

702. Sensitivity analysis -which risks will have the most impact on the Sales Strategy project?

703. Degree of confidence in estimated size estimate?

704. Can you handle the investment risk?

705. How carefully have the potential competitors been identified?

706. What are the risks involved in appointing external agencies to manage the Sales Strategy project?

707. What are the levels of understanding of the future users of this technology?

708. What are its business ethics?

709. Do others match with the clients requirement?

710. What will be the likely incidence of conflict with neighboring Sales Strategy projects?

711. Can you avoid altogether some things that might go wrong?

712. The customer requests a change to the Sales Strategy project that would increase the Sales Strategy project risk. Which should you do before ass the others?

2.35 Risk Data Sheet: Sales Strategy

713. What are the main threats to your existence?

714. How can hazards be reduced?

715. What will be the consequences if it happens?

716. Type of risk identified?

717. What is the environment within which you operate (social trends, economic, community values, broad based participation, national directions etc.)?

718. Who has a vested interest in how you perform as your organization (our stakeholders)?

719. What will be the consequences if the risk happens?

720. What are your core values?

721. What are you weak at and therefore need to do better?

722. What actions can be taken to eliminate or remove risk?

723. Is the data sufficiently specified in terms of the type of failure being analyzed, and its frequency or probability?

724. What are you trying to achieve (Objectives)?

725. Do effective diagnostic tests exist?

726. How reliable is the data source?

727. What can happen?

728. Potential for recurrence?

729. What can you do?

730. During work activities could hazards exist?

2.36 Procurement Management Plan: Sales Strategy

731. Similar Sales Strategy projects?

732. Are Sales Strategy project team members involved in detailed estimating and scheduling?

733. Has a structured approach been used to break work effort into manageable components (WBS)?

734. Sales Strategy project Objectives?

735. Has a sponsor been identified?

736. Is there a procurement management plan in place?

737. Are changes in deliverable commitments agreed to by all affected groups & individuals?

738. Based on your Sales Strategy project communication management plan, what worked well?

739. Is there an on-going process in place to monitor Sales Strategy project risks?

740. What areas are overlooked on this Sales Strategy project?

741. Are the people assigned to the Sales Strategy project sufficiently qualified?

742. Are meeting objectives identified for each meeting?

743. Public engagement – did you get it right?

744. Are there checklists created to determine if all quality processes are followed?

745. What areas does the group agree are the biggest success on the Sales Strategy project?

746. Have all necessary approvals been obtained?

747. Is the steering committee active in Sales Strategy project oversight?

748. Is the schedule updated on a periodic basis?

749. How will you coordinate Procurement with aspects of the Sales Strategy project?

2.37 Source Selection Criteria: Sales Strategy

750. Who must be notified?

751. Can you make a cost/technical tradeoff?

752. How will you evaluate offerors proposals?

753. What should be considered when developing evaluation standards?

754. What documentation is necessary regarding electronic communications?

755. How are clarifications and communications appropriately used?

756. Do you ensure you evaluate what you asked for, not what you want to see or expect to see?

757. How important is cost in the source selection decision relative to past performance and technical considerations?

758. Is this a cost contract?

759. Are there any common areas of weaknesses or deficiencies in the proposals in the competitive range?

760. How can business terms and conditions be improved to yield more effective price competition?

761. What should a Draft Request for Proposal (DRFP) include?

762. How and when do you enter into Sales Strategy project Procurement Management?

763. What should clarifications include?

764. How do you manage procurement?

765. Do you consider all weaknesses, significant weaknesses, and deficiencies?

766. What does an evaluation address and what does a sample resemble?

767. What past performance information should be requested?

768. When must you conduct a debriefing?

769. What will you use to capture evaluation and subsequent documentation?

2.38 Stakeholder Management Plan: Sales Strategy

770. Are schedule deliverables actually delivered?

771. Are enough systems & user personnel assigned to the Sales Strategy project?

772. Why would a customer be interested in a particular product or service?

773. Are parking lot items captured?

774. What process was used to identify risks to the Sales Strategy projects success?

775. Which risks pose the highest threat?

776. How are stakeholders chosen and what roles might they have on a Sales Strategy project?

777. What action will be taken once reports have been received?

778. Have process improvement efforts been completed before requirements efforts begin?

779. Has your organization readiness assessment been conducted?

780. Was the scope definition used in task sequencing?

781. If a problem has been detected, what tools can be used to determine a root cause?

782. Have the key elements of a coherent Sales Strategy project management strategy been established?

783. How many Sales Strategy project staff does this specific process affect?

784. What information should be collected?

785. Are there unnecessary steps that are creating bottlenecks and/or causing people to wait?

2.39 Change Management Plan: Sales Strategy

786. What work practices will be affected?

787. Has a training need analysis been carried out?

788. Who should be involved in developing a change management strategy?

789. What tasks are needed?

790. What relationships will change?

791. Who might be able to help you the most?

792. Who will fund the training?

793. What are the dependencies?

794. What are the needs, priorities and special interests of the audience?

795. Has the training provider been established?

796. Is there support for this application(s) and are the details available for distribution?

797. What new behaviours are required?

798. What new competencies will be required for the roles?

799. How much change management is needed?

800. Has the target training audience been identified and nominated?

801. What risks may occur upfront?

802. Are work location changes required?

803. Have the systems been configured and tested?

804. Do you need a new organizational structure?

3.0 Executing Process Group: Sales Strategy

805. Why is it important to determine activity sequencing on Sales Strategy projects?

806. What will you do to minimize the impact should a risk event occur?

807. Is activity definition the first process involved in Sales Strategy project time management?

808. How does a Sales Strategy project life cycle differ from a product life cycle?

809. Is the Sales Strategy project making progress in helping to achieve the set results?

810. What are the Sales Strategy project management deliverables of each process group?

811. What is in place for ensuring adequate change control on Sales Strategy projects that involve outside contracts?

812. On which process should team members spend the most time?

813. How well defined and documented were the Sales Strategy project management processes you chose to use?

814. How do you control progress of your Sales

Strategy project?

815. Would you rate yourself as being risk-averse, risk-neutral, or risk-seeking?

816. Do Sales Strategy project managers understand your organizational context for Sales Strategy projects?

817. What communication items need improvement?

818. How does the job market and current state of the economy affect human resource management?

819. How could you control progress of your Sales Strategy project?

820. How do you measure difficulty?

821. What are the main parts of the scope statement?

822. What is the shortest possible time it will take to complete this Sales Strategy project?

823. When is the appropriate time to bring the scorecard to Board meetings?

3.1 Team Member Status Report: Sales Strategy

824. How does this product, good, or service meet the needs of the Sales Strategy project and your organization as a whole?

825. How can you make it practical?

826. Are the products of your organizations Sales Strategy projects meeting customers objectives?

827. Do you have an Enterprise Sales Strategy project Management Office (EPMO)?

828. How it is to be done?

829. Why is it to be done?

830. What is to be done?

831. Does your organization have the means (staff, money, contract, etc.) to produce or to acquire the product, good, or service?

832. What specific interest groups do you have in place?

833. Are your organizations Sales Strategy projects more successful over time?

834. How much risk is involved?

835. The problem with Reward & Recognition Programs is that the truly deserving people all too often get left out. How can you make it practical?

836. Are the attitudes of staff regarding Sales Strategy project work improving?

837. Will the staff do training or is that done by a third party?

838. How will resource planning be done?

839. Does the product, good, or service already exist within your organization?

840. Is there evidence that staff is taking a more professional approach toward management of your organizations Sales Strategy projects?

841. Does every department have to have a Sales Strategy project Manager on staff?

842. When a teams productivity and success depend on collaboration and the efficient flow of information, what generally fails them?

3.2 Change Request: Sales Strategy

843. What are the basic mechanics of the Change Advisory Board (CAB)?

844. What is the relationship between requirements attributes and reliability?

845. Are there requirements attributes that are strongly related to the complexity and size?

846. How fast will change requests be approved?

847. Where do changes come from?

848. What is the purpose of change control?

849. What is the relationship between requirements attributes and attributes like complexity and size?

850. Why were your requested changes rejected or not made?

851. Will all change requests and current status be logged?

852. Does the schedule include Sales Strategy project management time and change request analysis time?

853. Have scm procedures for noting the change, recording it, and reporting it been followed?

854. What is the function of the change control committee?

855. Will there be a change request form in use?

856. How many times must the change be modified or presented to the change control board before it is approved?

857. What needs to be communicated?

858. What are the requirements for urgent changes?

859. What should be regulated in a change control operating instruction?

860. What has an inspector to inspect and to check?

861. Who is responsible to authorize changes?

862. Who needs to approve change requests?

3.3 Change Log: Sales Strategy

863. Will the Sales Strategy project fail if the change request is not executed?

864. How does this change affect the timeline of the schedule?

865. Is the change backward compatible without limitations?

866. Is the submitted change a new change or a modification of a previously approved change?

867. When was the request approved?

868. How does this relate to the standards developed for specific business processes?

869. Is the requested change request a result of changes in other Sales Strategy project(s)?

870. Who initiated the change request?

871. How does this change affect scope?

872. When was the request submitted?

873. Is the change request within Sales Strategy project scope?

874. Do the described changes impact on the integrity or security of the system?

875. Is the change request open, closed or pending?

876. Is this a mandatory replacement?

877. Does the suggested change request represent a desired enhancement to the products functionality?

3.4 Decision Log: Sales Strategy

878. How does provision of information, both in terms of content and presentation, influence acceptance of alternative strategies?

879. Decision-making process; how will the team make decisions?

880. At what point in time does loss become unacceptable?

881. How do you know when you are achieving it?

882. Is your opponent open to a non-traditional workflow, or will it likely challenge anything you do?

883. Does anything need to be adjusted?

884. What is the line where eDiscovery ends and document review begins?

885. Meeting purpose; why does this team meet?

886. Behaviors; what are guidelines that the team has identified that will assist them with getting the most out of team meetings?

887. Is everything working as expected?

888. Who is the decisionmaker?

889. What was the rationale for the decision?

890. With whom was the decision shared or considered?

891. Linked to original objective?

892. Adversarial environment. is your opponent open to a non-traditional workflow, or will it likely challenge anything you do?

893. Do strategies and tactics aimed at less than full control reduce the costs of management or simply shift the cost burden?

894. How do you define success?

895. What eDiscovery problem or issue did your organization set out to fix or make better?

896. How effective is maintaining the log at facilitating organizational learning?

897. What alternatives/risks were considered?

3.5 Quality Audit: Sales Strategy

898. How does your organization know that the system for managing its facilities is appropriately effective and constructive?

899. Are all records associated with the reconditioning of a device maintained for a minimum of two years after the sale or disposal of the last device within a lot of merchandise?

900. Health and safety arrangements; stress management workshops. How does your organization know that it provides a safe and healthy environment?

901. How does your organization know that its staff have appropriate access to a fair and effective grievance process?

902. Does your organization have set of goals, objectives, strategies and targets that are clearly understood by the Board and staff?

903. How does the organization know that its industry and community engagement planning and management systems are appropriately effective and constructive in enabling relationships with key stakeholder groups?

904. How does your organization know that its planning processes are appropriately effective and constructive?

905. How are you auditing your organizations

compliance with regulations?

906. Are all areas associated with the storage and reconditioning of devices clean, free of rubbish, adequately ventilated and in good repair?

907. How does your organization know that its relationships with industry and employers are appropriately effective and constructive?

908. How does your organization know that its system for attending to the health and wellbeing of its staff is appropriately effective and constructive?

909. How does your organization know that its system for recruiting the best staff possible are appropriately effective and constructive?

910. Does the report read coherently?

911. Can your organization demonstrate exactly how and why results were achieved?

912. How does your organization know that its system for supporting staff research capability is appropriately effective and constructive?

913. How does your organization ensure that equipment is appropriately maintained and producing valid results?

914. Is your organizations resource allocation system properly aligned with its collection of intentions?

915. How well do you think your organization engages with the outside community?

916. Are all complaints involving the possible failure of a device, labeling, or packaging to meet any of its specifications reviewed, evaluated, and investigated?

917. How does your organization know that its staff support services planning and management systems are appropriately effective and constructive?

3.6 Team Directory: Sales Strategy

918. Who will be the stakeholders on your next Sales Strategy project?

919. Who are your stakeholders (customers, sponsors, end users, team members)?

920. Process decisions: which organizational elements and which individuals will be assigned management functions?

921. How will you accomplish and manage the objectives?

922. Decisions: what could be done better to improve the quality of the constructed product?

923. Contract requirements complied with?

924. When will you produce deliverables?

925. Who is the Sponsor?

926. Process decisions: do invoice amounts match accepted work in place?

927. Is construction on schedule?

928. Who are the Team Members?

929. Process decisions: are contractors adequately prosecuting the work?

930. Process decisions: do job conditions warrant additional actions to collect job information and document on-site activity?

931. What are you going to deliver or accomplish?

932. Why is the work necessary?

933. Timing: when do the effects of communication take place?

934. Who will write the meeting minutes and distribute?

935. How do unidentified risks impact the outcome of the Sales Strategy project?

3.7 Team Operating Agreement: Sales Strategy

936. Did you prepare participants for the next meeting?

937. Are there influences outside the team that may affect performance, and if so, have you identified and addressed them?

938. What are some potential sources of conflict among team members?

939. Do team members reside in more than two countries?

940. What is culture?

941. Do you leverage technology engagement tools group chat, polls, screen sharing, etc.?

942. Do you ask participants to close laptops and place mobile devices on silent on the table while the meeting is in progress?

943. Resource allocation: how will individual team members account for time and expenses, and how will this be allocated in the team budget?

944. Seconds for members to respond?

945. Must your team members rely on the expertise of other members to complete tasks?

946. Do you determine the meeting length and time of day?

947. Confidentiality: how will confidential information be handled?

948. What individual strengths does each team member bring to the group?

949. Do you record meetings for the already stated unable to attend?

950. Do you post any action items, due dates, and responsibilities on the team website?

951. How will your group handle planned absences?

952. Did you delegate tasks such as taking meeting minutes, presenting a topic and soliciting input?

953. Do you ensure that all participants know how to use the required technology?

954. How does teaming fit in with overall organizational goals and meet organizational needs?

955. Did you draft the meeting agenda?

3.8 Team Performance Assessment: Sales Strategy

956. To what degree can team members frequently and easily communicate with one another?

957. What makes opportunities more or less obvious?

958. To what degree can the team measure progress against specific goals?

959. To what degree are the members clear on what they are individually responsible for and what they are jointly responsible for?

960. To what degree do team members frequently explore the teams purpose and its implications?

961. How do you recognize and praise members for contributions?

962. Is there a particular method of data analysis that you would recommend as a means of demonstrating that method variance is not of great concern for a given dataset?

963. To what degree can team members meet frequently enough to accomplish the teams ends?

964. Does more radicalness mean more perceived benefits?

965. To what degree does the teams approach to its

work allow for modification and improvement over time?

966. To what degree will the team ensure that all members equitably share the work essential to the success of the team?

967. To what degree does the teams work approach provide opportunity for members to engage in fact-based problem solving?

968. Individual task proficiency and team process behavior: what is important for team functioning?

969. To what degree do team members agree with the goals, relative importance, and the ways in which achievement will be measured?

970. Where to from here?

971. To what degree are staff involved as partners in the improvement process?

972. To what degree are the relative importance and priority of the goals clear to all team members?

973. To what degree will the approach capitalize on and enhance the skills of all team members in a manner that takes into consideration other demands on members of the team?

974. To what degree does the teams purpose constitute a broader, deeper aspiration than just accomplishing short-term goals?

975. If you are worried about method variance before

you collect data, what sort of design elements might you include to reduce or eliminate the threat of method variance?

3.9 Team Member Performance Assessment: Sales Strategy

976. How do you start collaborating?

977. Does statute or regulation require the job responsibility?

978. What are top priorities?

979. Verify business objectives. Are they appropriate, and well-articulated?

980. How does your team work together?

981. What qualities does a successful Team leader possess?

982. How will they be formed?

983. To what degree does the teams purpose contain themes that are particularly meaningful and memorable?

984. To what degree is there a sense that only the team can succeed?

985. Are the draft goals SMART ?

986. To what degree do team members articulate the teams work approach?

987. How do you create a self-sustaining capacity for a

collaborative culture?

988. What were the challenges that resulted for training and assessment?

989. What changes do you need to make to align practices with beliefs?

990. Why do performance reviews?

991. What are the standards or expectations for success?

992. To what degree are the goals realistic?

993. What are the staffs preferences for training on technology-based platforms?

3.10 Issue Log: Sales Strategy

994. What effort will a change need?

995. How do you manage communications?

996. How much time does it take to do it?

997. Do you feel a register helps?

998. Who reported the issue?

999. What are the typical contents?

1000. Who are the members of the governing body?

1001. Are you constantly rushing from meeting to meeting?

1002. How do you reply to this question; you am new here and managing this major program. How do you suggest you build your network?

1003. What steps can you take for positive relationships?

1004. Is the issue log kept in a safe place?

1005. Who is the stakeholder?

1006. Can an impact cause deviation beyond team, stage or Sales Strategy project tolerances?

1007. How do you manage human resources?

4.0 Monitoring and Controlling Process Group: Sales Strategy

1008. Do the partners have sufficient financial capacity to keep up the benefits produced by the programme?

1009. How many potential communications channels exist on the Sales Strategy project?

1010. In what way has the program come up with innovative measures for problem-solving?

1011. How is Agile Sales Strategy project Management done?

1012. Who needs to be involved in the planning?

1013. Propriety: who needs to be involved in the evaluation to be ethical?

1014. Were decisions made in a timely manner?

1015. How are you doing?

1016. Is there adequate validation on required fields?

1017. Is there sufficient funding available for this?

1018. What is the timeline?

1019. Is there undesirable impact on staff or resources?

1020. Just how important is your work to the overall success of the Sales Strategy project?

1021. Are there areas that need improvement?

1022. What are the goals of the program?

1023. How is agile portfolio management done?

1024. Where is the Risk in the Sales Strategy project?

1025. What departments are involved in its daily operation?

4.1 Project Performance Report: Sales Strategy

1026. To what degree can all members engage in open and interactive considerations?

1027. To what degree will team members, individually and collectively, commit time to help themselves and others learn and develop skills?

1028. To what degree are the structures of the formal organization consistent with the behaviors in the informal organization?

1029. To what degree do the relationships of the informal organization motivate taskrelevant behavior and facilitate task completion?

1030. To what degree do the goals specify concrete team work products?

1031. To what degree do members articulate the goals beyond the team membership?

1032. To what degree do individual skills and abilities match task demands?

1033. To what degree does the teams work approach provide opportunity for members to engage in open interaction?

1034. To what degree can the team ensure that all members are individually and jointly accountable for the teams purpose, goals, approach, and work-products?

1035. What is the degree to which rules govern information exchange between individuals within your organization?

1036. To what degree are the teams goals and objectives clear, simple, and measurable?

1037. To what degree does the team possess adequate membership to achieve its ends?

1038. To what degree are fresh input and perspectives systematically caught and added (for example, through information and analysis, new members, and senior sponsors)?

1039. To what degree do team members feel that the purpose of the team is important, if not exciting?

1040. To what degree do all members feel responsible for all agreed-upon measures?

4.2 Variance Analysis: Sales Strategy

1041. Is work progressively subdivided into detailed work packages as requirements are defined?

1042. Who are responsible for the establishment of budgets and assignment of resources for overhead performance?

1043. Is data disseminated to the contractors management timely, accurate, and usable?

1044. Did an existing competitor change strategy?

1045. What does a favorable labor efficiency variance mean?

1046. What is exceptional?

1047. Is work properly classified as measured effort, LOE, or apportioned effort and appropriately separated?

1048. Are data elements reconcilable between internal summary reports and reports forwarded to the stakeholders?

1049. What is the dollar amount of the fluctuation?

1050. Are the bases and rates for allocating costs from each indirect pool consistently applied?

1051. Is cost and schedule performance measurement done in a consistent, systematic manner?

1052. How have the setting and use of standards changed over time?

1053. Is the entire contract planned in time-phased control accounts to the extent practicable?

1054. Are indirect costs charged to the appropriate indirect pools and incurring organization?

1055. Are management actions taken to reduce indirect costs when there are significant adverse variances?

1056. Are control accounts opened and closed based on the start and completion of work contained therein?

1057. Why are standard cost systems used?

1058. How do you identify and isolate causes of favorable and unfavorable cost and schedule variances?

1059. Are the wbs and organizational levels for application of the Sales Strategy projected overhead costs identified?

4.3 Earned Value Status: Sales Strategy

1060. Earned value can be used in almost any Sales Strategy project situation and in almost any Sales Strategy project environment. it may be used on large Sales Strategy projects, medium sized Sales Strategy projects, tiny Sales Strategy projects (in cut-down form), complex and simple Sales Strategy projects and in any market sector. some people, of course, know all about earned value, they have used it for years - but perhaps not as effectively as they could have?

1061. Verification is a process of ensuring that the developed system satisfies the stakeholders agreements and specifications; Are you building the product right? What do you verify?

1062. How does this compare with other Sales Strategy projects?

1063. What is the unit of forecast value?

1064. Are you hitting your Sales Strategy projects targets?

1065. If earned value management (EVM) is so good in determining the true status of a Sales Strategy project and Sales Strategy project its completion, why is it that hardly any one uses it in information systems related Sales Strategy projects?

1066. Where is evidence-based earned value in your

organization reported?

1067. Where are your problem areas?

1068. Validation is a process of ensuring that the developed system will actually achieve the stakeholders desired outcomes; Are you building the right product? What do you validate?

1069. How much is it going to cost by the finish?

1070. When is it going to finish?

4.4 Risk Audit: Sales Strategy

1071. What risk does not having unique identification present?

1072. Do end-users have realistic expectations?

1073. Are regular safety inspections made of buildings, grounds and equipment?

1074. How effective are your risk controls?

1075. Is all expenditure authorised through an identified process?

1076. Do you record and file all audits?

1077. Are all financial transactions accurately recorded (receipted, banked)?

1078. Are the software tools integrated with each other?

1079. Is safety information provided to all involved?

1080. Do requirements demand the use of new analysis, design, or testing methods?

1081. What are risks and how do you manage them?

1082. What is the implication of budget constraint on this process?

1083. How do you manage risk?

1084. Are requirements fully understood by the team and customers?

1085. If applicable; which route/packaging option do you choose for transport of hazmat material?

1086. Is a software Sales Strategy project management tool available?

1087. Improving fraud detection: do auditors react to abnormal inconsistencies between financial and non-financial measures?

1088. What impact does prior experience have on decisions made during the risk-assessment process?

1089. Has everyone (staff, volunteers and participants) agreed to a code of behaviour or conduct?

1090. Are all participants informed of safety issues?

4.5 Contractor Status Report: Sales Strategy

1091. What was the actual budget or estimated cost for your organizations services?

1092. What is the average response time for answering a support call?

1093. What was the overall budget or estimated cost?

1094. Describe how often regular updates are made to the proposed solution. Are corresponding regular updates included in the standard maintenance plan?

1095. How does the proposed individual meet each requirement?

1096. What are the minimum and optimal bandwidth requirements for the proposed solution?

1097. If applicable; describe your standard schedule for new software version releases. Are new software version releases included in the standard maintenance plan?

1098. What was the final actual cost?

1099. Who can list a Sales Strategy project as organization experience, your organization or a previous employee of your organization?

1100. Are there contractual transfer concerns?

1101. What was the budget or estimated cost for your organizations services?

1102. What process manages the contracts?

1103. How is risk transferred?

1104. How long have you been using the services?

4.6 Formal Acceptance: Sales Strategy

1105. Was the Sales Strategy project work done on time, within budget, and according to specification?

1106. How well did the team follow the methodology?

1107. What lessons were learned about your Sales Strategy project management methodology?

1108. Was the client satisfied with the Sales Strategy project results?

1109. Was the Sales Strategy project goal achieved?

1110. Do you buy-in installation services?

1111. What features, practices, and processes proved to be strengths or weaknesses?

1112. What was done right?

1113. Was business value realized?

1114. Who would use it?

1115. Who supplies data?

1116. What are the requirements against which to test, Who will execute?

1117. Was the sponsor/customer satisfied?

1118. What is the Acceptance Management Process?

1119. Do you buy pre-configured systems or build your own configuration?

1120. What function(s) does it fill or meet?

1121. General estimate of the costs and times to complete the Sales Strategy project?

1122. Is formal acceptance of the Sales Strategy project product documented and distributed?

1123. Have all comments been addressed?

1124. Do you perform formal acceptance or burn-in tests?

5.0 Closing Process Group: Sales Strategy

1125. Did you do things well?

1126. How well did the chosen processes produce the expected results?

1127. How well defined and documented were the Sales Strategy project management processes you chose to use?

1128. Who are the Sales Strategy project stakeholders?

1129. What is the overall risk of the Sales Strategy project to your organization?

1130. Is the Sales Strategy project funded?

1131. Is there a clear cause and effect between the activity and the lesson learned?

1132. Were the outcomes different from the already stated planned?

1133. Did the Sales Strategy project team have enough people to execute the Sales Strategy project plan?

1134. What could be done to improve the process?

1135. What is an Encumbrance?

1136. How will staff learn how to use the deliverables?

1137. How well did the chosen processes fit the needs of the Sales Strategy project?

1138. Did the Sales Strategy project management methodology work?

1139. Was the user/client satisfied with the end product?

5.1 Procurement Audit: Sales Strategy

1140. Does the department have a procurement strategy and is it implemented?

1141. Were calculations used in evaluation adequate and correct?

1142. Was timely and equal access to contract documents and information provided to all candidates?

1143. Are reports based on sound data available to the already stated responsible for monitoring the performance of contracts?

1144. Are requisitions and other purchase requests batched to reduce the number of orders issued?

1145. Is the procurement process fully digitalized?

1146. Was the award criteria that of the most economically advantageous tender?

1147. Is there no evidence of any external or superior pressure to reach a specific result?

1148. Do all requests for materials, supplies, and services require supervisors authorization?

1149. What are the threats to supplier relations?

1150. Are required quality and service standards set?

1151. Were there no inconsistencies between the several tender documents?

1152. Is it clear which procurement procedure your organization has opted for?

1153. Are the rules for automatic payment in computer programs approved by management prior to implementation?

1154. Are obtained prices/qualities competitive to prices/qualities obtained by other procurement functions/units, comparing obtained or improved value for money?

1155. Are contract changes after awarding properly justified and executed?

1156. Are there appropriate controls in place to ensure that the procurement Sales Strategy project complies with relevant legislation?

1157. Are there complementary rules to be used and are they applied?

1158. Has your organization clearly defined the award criteria?

1159. How do you address the risk of fraud and corruption?

5.2 Contract Close-Out: Sales Strategy

1160. How does it work?

1161. Have all contracts been completed?

1162. Was the contract type appropriate?

1163. Have all acceptance criteria been met prior to final payment to contractors?

1164. Parties: who is involved?

1165. Was the contract complete without requiring numerous changes and revisions?

1166. What happens to the recipient of services?

1167. Have all contract records been included in the Sales Strategy project archives?

1168. How/when used ?

1169. Was the contract sufficiently clear so as not to result in numerous disputes and misunderstandings?

1170. Change in attitude or behavior?

1171. Are the signers the authorized officials?

1172. Change in circumstances?

1173. Have all contracts been closed?

1174. Change in knowledge?

1175. How is the contracting office notified of the automatic contract close-out?

1176. Parties: Authorized?

1177. What is capture management?

1178. Has each contract been audited to verify acceptance and delivery?

5.3 Project or Phase Close-Out: Sales Strategy

1179. Does the lesson describe a function that would be done differently the next time?

1180. Who is responsible for award close-out?

1181. Does the lesson educate others to improve performance?

1182. What is this stakeholder expecting?

1183. What are the mandatory communication needs for each stakeholder?

1184. Who exerted influence that has positively affected or negatively impacted the Sales Strategy project?

1185. Did the Sales Strategy project management methodology work?

1186. Who are the Sales Strategy project stakeholders and what are roles and involvement?

1187. What were the actual outcomes?

1188. In addition to assessing whether the Sales Strategy project was successful, it is equally critical to analyze why it was or was not fully successful. Are you including this?

1189. Did the delivered product meet the specified requirements and goals of the Sales Strategy project?

1190. What are they?

1191. What could have been improved?

1192. What security considerations needed to be addressed during the procurement life cycle?

1193. What are the marketing communication needs for each stakeholder?

1194. Have business partners been involved extensively, and what data was required for them?

1195. What was the preferred delivery mechanism?

5.4 Lessons Learned: Sales Strategy

1196. What are the skills directly related to the task?

1197. How actively and meaningfully were stakeholders involved in the Sales Strategy project?

1198. Are new goals needed?

1199. Was the change control process properly implemented to manage changes to cost, scope, schedule, or quality?

1200. For the next Sales Strategy project, how could you improve on the way Sales Strategy project was conducted?

1201. What are the Benefits of Measurements?

1202. How well do you feel the executives supported this Sales Strategy project?

1203. How effective was the acceptance management process?

1204. How spontaneous are the communications?

1205. Is there any way in which you think your development process hampered this Sales Strategy project?

1206. Did the Sales Strategy project management methodology work?

1207. Do you have any real problems?

1208. Were the right people available when required?

1209. How effective was the support you received during implementation of the product/service?

1210. How effective were the techniques used to prepare you and your organization for the impact of the changes brought about by the product or service produced by the Sales Strategy project?

1211. How useful was your testing?

1212. What were the challenges and pitfalls?

1213. Will the information remain current?

1214. What would you like to see better documented about how to use existing processes on this type of Sales Strategy project?

1215. Were any objectives unmet?

Index

267

control 2, 37, 48, 69, 89-91, 93, 95-96, 99-100, 126, 131, 140, 152-153, 169, 173-174, 178, 188-189, 214-215, 218-219, 223, 242, 259
controlled   59, 174
controls   16, 60, 67, 78, 81, 89-90, 93, 96-97, 100, 163, 198, 245, 254
convention   117
conversion   148
convey   1
cooperate   178
coordinate   207
Copyright   1
correct 42, 89, 136, 172, 193, 253
corrective   44, 91, 139, 192, 198
correlate   184
correspond   8-9, 153
corruption   254
cosmetic   148
costing 177
counting   121, 141
countries   229
counts 121
course 40, 49, 243
covering   8, 95
coworker   106
crashing   164
craziest   104
create 17, 69, 121, 123-124, 146, 169, 234
created   58, 91, 130, 133, 137, 155, 207
creating   7, 54, 133, 211
creative   20
creativity   78
credible   178
crisis   25
criteria 2, 4, 8-9, 32, 36, 66, 76, 80-81, 98, 104, 115, 125-126, 141, 144, 147, 169, 179-180, 208, 253-255
CRITERION   2, 15, 26, 42, 57, 73, 89, 102
critical 28, 31, 33, 58, 76, 93, 97, 119, 138, 148, 153, 157, 161, 257
cross-sell   110
crucial 64, 131
crystal 10
culture 31, 63, 155, 184, 190-191, 193, 229, 235
current 29, 42, 47, 58, 60-61, 68, 80, 93, 105, 107, 110-111, 148, 163, 187, 189-190, 198-199, 202, 215, 218, 260

honest 104
humans 7
hypotheses 57
identified 1, 17-18, 24, 38-39, 61-62, 68-69, 74, 138-139, 143,
147, 152-153, 159, 185, 190-191, 193, 198-200, 202, 204, 206-207,
213, 222, 229, 242, 245
identify9-10, 19, 21, 25, 67, 70, 78, 131, 146, 152, 178, 188-189,
194, 210, 242
ignore 19
ignoring 119
images142
imbedded 92
Immediate 131-132
impact4, 39, 42, 46, 48-49, 51-52, 54, 86, 131, 174, 180, 196, 198-
200, 202, 214, 220, 228, 236-237, 246, 260
impacted 44, 148, 257
impacts 46, 55, 148, 171
implement 18, 42, 62, 89, 188
implicit115
importance 232
important 19, 30, 58-59, 61, 104, 106, 116, 120, 122, 128,
166, 182, 185, 188, 208, 214, 232, 238, 240
improve 2, 9, 62, 73, 75-79, 82-87, 128, 185, 188, 227, 251,
257, 259
improved 78, 80, 82, 86, 95, 134, 208, 254, 258
improving 73, 217, 246
inbound 113
incentives 99
incidence 203
include 74, 84, 137, 153, 209, 218, 233
included 2, 7, 15, 48, 142-143, 170, 178, 247, 255
INCLUDES 9
including 17, 28, 31, 36, 51, 53, 59, 93-95, 148, 257
increase 82, 104, 201, 203
increasing 111
incurred 46
Incurrence 153
incurring 153, 242
in-depth 8, 10
indicate 70, 98, 104
indicated 91
indicators 24, 54-55, 58, 61, 63, 69, 95, 134, 152-153, 200
indirect 53, 153, 176, 241-242

management 1, 3-5, 8-9, 18-19, 23, 31, 36, 38, 46, 57-58, 63, 71-72, 74-75, 80, 82, 84-86, 104, 110, 118, 126, 131, 133, 136-140, 147-149, 152-153, 155, 159, 168-170, 172, 174, 176, 180, 182, 188-189, 192, 194, 196-201, 206, 209-218, 223-224, 226-227, 237-238, 241-243, 246, 249, 251-252, 254, 256-257, 259
manager   7, 9, 25, 28, 37, 116, 138, 169, 188, 193, 217
managers   2, 125, 127, 168, 192, 215
manages   75, 248
managing   2, 77, 125, 130, 224, 236
mandatory   221, 257
manner   15, 84, 152, 174, 232, 237, 241
mantle 112
mapped   27
Mapping   58, 63-64
market 17, 131, 161, 215, 243
marketer   7
marketing   111, 258
markets   20
Master 172
material   161, 184, 246
materials   1, 146, 253
matrices   144
Matrix 2-4, 131, 144, 188, 202
matter 37, 54-55
mature 140, 189
maximizing   124
maximum   127
meaningful   50, 109, 153, 234
measurable   30, 32, 153, 240
measure   2, 9, 16, 23, 33, 35, 42-45, 47-49, 51-52, 55, 57, 59, 73, 76, 78, 81, 87, 94, 96-98, 100, 131, 134, 178-179, 182, 184, 202, 215, 231
measured   21, 43, 45, 47, 49, 52, 54, 76, 94, 182, 232, 241
measures   46, 48, 53-54, 58-59, 61, 69, 71, 91, 95, 98, 134, 198, 237, 240, 246
measuring   153
mechanical   1
mechanics   218
mechanism   258
mechanisms   146, 187
medium   243
meeting   34, 37, 96, 146, 190, 207, 216, 222, 228-230, 236
meetings   26-27, 31, 41, 146, 155, 193, 215, 222, 230

CPSIA information can be obtained
at www.ICGtesting.com
Printed in the USA
BVHW082019110819
555624BV00016BA/1882/P